Comfortable
American Homes

Comfortable American Homes

Laughter in the kitchen. Peaceful moments of solitude on a front porch. The ease of daily living in a smartly designed home. Each is a simple pleasure that brings comfort to our day-to-day lives. And as we plan to build a new home, these are a few of the things we hope to find within the sheltering space of newly constructed walls.

Comfortable American Homes welcomes you to a carefully selected presentation of 186 home plans – each one designed with comfortable living in mind. So whether you're looking for a spacious design for a growing family, or a smaller home that will fit nicely on a narrow lot, the following pages will provide a wide variety of comfortable home plans from today's most sought-after architects and designers.

Comfortable American Homes

CONTENTS

above Our cover plan, number 32114, is featured on **page 146**.

below Windows lining this kitchen sink to brighten up the room can be viewed in one of our Farmhouse Favorites on **page 50**.

FIND THOUSANDS OF PLANS ON-LINE AT WWW.FAMILYHOMEPLANS.COM

Plan 99431, page 145.

Plan 32114, page 147.

Plan 32056, page 55.

Comfortable American Homes

AN ACTIVE INTEREST MEDIA
PUBLICATION

GARLINGHOUSE, LLC

General Manager & Publisher	Marie L. Galastro
Art Director	Christopher Berrien
Managing Editor	Debra Cochran
Art Production Manager	Debra Novitch
Production Artist	Cindy King

National Sales Director	Bruce Arant
Director of Plan Sales	Kris Sbarra
Telesales Representatives	Jessica Salazar
	Timothy A. Bowker
	Nicole Clairborne-Small
Customer Service Representative	Rita Humphries
Accounting	Monika Jackson
Office Manager	Christine J. Monteleone
Fulfillment Manager	Tammy Clark

For Plan Orders in United States
4125 Lafayette Center Drive, Suite 100
Chantilly, VA 20151
1-800-235-5700
Fax: 703-222-9705

For Plan Orders in Canada
The Garlinghouse Company
102 Ellis Street, Penticton, BC V2A 4L5
1-800-361-7526

Newsstand Distributor
Curtis Circulation Company
730 River Road, New Milford, New Jersey 07646
Phone: 201-634-7400 Fax: 201-634-7499

ACTIVE INTEREST MEDIA

President and CEO	Efrem Zimbalist III
Group Publisher and COO	Andrew W. Clurman
Senior VP, Chief Financial Officer	Mitchell Faigen
Senior VP, Circulation, Production, and Operations	Patricia B. Fox

began to see that as much as they liked the home's design, certain rooms and windows were not positioned to appreciate the coveted watery vista.

Realizing that specific modifications were necessary before the house could become a riverfront reality, the Heims called a customer service representative at The Garlinghouse Company at 800-235-5700. They knew that in addition to providing quality home plans, Garlinghouse also helps buyers personalize their plans to perfection by offering design modification services. The Heim's concerns were soon put to rest as they shared their vision of how the design might take full advantage of its scenic surroundings.

A Home the Heims' Way

A careful assessment of the Heims' desire for scenic vistas from inside the home brought about a number of fundamental alterations to the plan. To start, the garage was relocated from the waterfront side to the street side, without sacrificing any valuable car and storage space. The entrance to the full daylight basement was changed to the rear of the house.

Once the waterfront side of the plan was cleared, an airy covered porch was added. Embracing three sides of the house, the porch imparts an idyllic view of the river and wooded surroundings. For its ability to capitalize on the exquisite vista, these plans get an "A-plus" for performance. Inside, rooms actually trade places, with the kitchen, cozy breakfast area and family room now owning the gorgeous view of the outdoors, while the main entry hall goes gracefully to the side street. For additional convenience and practicality, the laundry facility and half-bath are also relocated to the opposite side of the house.

The bright family room with fireplace is a cozy retreat in itself, moving temptingly to the kitchen and dining room, or just as easily onto the open-air porch.

The Heim's worked long and

above The key to successful plan modification is communication between you and the designer performing the changes.
You may discover that customization services are so affordable, that you'll opt to make more changes than originally anticipated.

hard for their priceless panorama and enjoying it from the bedroom window was essential. With this in mind, the spacious master suite was also strategically relocated.

Plan Modification FAQs

With thoughtful planning and help from The Garlinghouse Company, the stock plan the Heims chose was soon transformed into their dream home. Many, however, may ask: "How are plan modifications done?" "Is modifying a home plan expensive?" "Is it a complicated process?"

First, state-of-the-art computer technology and CAD (Computer Aided Design) drafting services make it possible to modify, redesign and renovate existing home stock plans, more quickly and efficiently than ever. Of

MODIFIED PLAN

FIRST FLOOR

SECOND FLOOR

above: State-of-the-art computer technology and CAD (Computer Aided Design) drafting services make it possible to modify, redesign and renovate existing home stock plans, more quickly and efficiently than ever.

course, the key to successful plan modification is communication between you and the designer performing the changes. Here's where you can help the most, by sharing the details of what you most desire to make your chosen stock plan, your dream plan.

The prices are set according to the challenge the design alteration presents. Modifications are either major or minor. It's that simple. If the structure of your home plan requires major modification in order to support the custom changes requested, the price will be reflected. For instance, adding a garage may in-

crease/decrease the square footage of a room. In that case, more design expertise is employed and the price of that custom alteration will be greater, but still impressively affordable.

Minor modifications include adding windows or moving doors. These alterations require less design input and as a result cost less.

You may discover that customization services are so affordable, that you'll opt to make more changes than originally anticipated. For example, adding the soaring ceiling you've always admired is no longer cost prohibi-

tive. Prices range from $240-$440. If having more than one fireplace is on your wish list, these prices make it possible, from $80-$180.

A Home to Call Your Own
Like Jay and Anna Heim, you too may one day view beautiful vistas from the comfort of your new home — with the style that's uniquely yours. It's easy with help from your friends at The Garlinghouse Company. We've been helping people build dreams since 1907. 🏛

Quick and Easy Customizing
Make Changes to Your Home Plan in 4 Easy Steps

Here's an **affordable** and **efficient** way to make **custom changes** to your home plan.

1 Select the house plan that most closely meets your needs. Purchase of a reproducible master (vellum) is necessary to make changes to a plan.

2 Call **800-235-5700** to place your order. Tell the sales representative you're interested in customizing a plan. A $50 refundable consultation fee will be charged. Then you'll need to complete a customization checklist indicating all the changes you wish to make to your plan, attaching sketches if necessary. If you proceed with the custom changes, the $50 will be credited to the total amount charged.

3 Fax the completed customization checklist to our design consultant at **1-866-477-5173** or e-mail **blarochelle@drummonddesigns.com**. Within 24 to 48* business hours you will be provided with a written cost estimate to modify your plan. Our design consultant will contact you by phone if you wish to discuss any of your changes in greater detail.

4 Once you approve the estimate, a 75% retainer fee is collected and customization work gets underway. Preliminary drawings can usually be completed within 5 to10* business days. Following approval of these preliminary drawings, your design changes are completed within 5 to 10* business days. Your remaining 25% balance due is collected prior to shipment of your completed drawings. You will be shipped five sets of revised blueprints, or a reproducible master.

*Terms are subject to change without notice.

BEFORE

AFTER

Sample Modification Pricing Guide

CATEGORIES	AVERAGE COST
Adding or removing living space (square footage)	Quote required
Adding or removing a garage	Starting at $400
Garage: Front entry to side load or vice versa	Starting at $300
Adding a screened porch	Starting at $280
Adding a bonus room in the attic	Starting at $450
Changing full basement to crawl space or vice versa	Starting at $495
Changing full basement to slab or vice versa	Starting at $495
Changing exterior building materials	Starting at $200
Changing roof lines	Starting at $360
Adjusting ceiling height	Starting at $280
Adding, moving or removing an exterior opening	$65 per opening
Adding or removing a fireplace	Starting at $90
Modifying a non-bearing wall or room	$65 per room
Changing exterior walls from 2"x4" to 2"x6"	Starting at $200
Redesigning a bathroom or a kitchen	Starting at $120
Reverse plan right reading	Quote required
Adapting plans for local building code requirements	Quote required
Adjust plan for handicapped accessibility	Quote required
Interactive Illustrations (choices of exterior materials)	Quote required
Metric conversion of home plan	Starting at $400

Note: Prices are subject to change according to plan size and style. Please remember that figures shown are average costs. Your quote may be higher or lower depending upon your specific requirements.

PHOTOGRAPHY: MAGGIE COLE

Custom FARMHOUSE

above A wraparound porch, tall brick chimney, forward-facing gables, and ample windows create a tasty country-style recipe for home.

below Deepened to provide extra shade during the hottest months, the wraparound porch has plenty of space for chairs and traffic circulation.

Built atop a hill, this home epitomizes farmhouse style: large windows to capture views, a deep wraparound porch, and a flowing floor plan with ample shared and private spaces. These owners customized their home by replacing the front first-floor windows with sliding doors, allowing breezes to flow throughout. Inside, a wall that separated the living and family rooms was removed, giving the open area access to the fireplace's light and views from the home's rear. The shared spaces are on the first floor. With the customized kitchen opening into the public rooms and the dining room separate and more formal, the home is perfect for entertaining. And if you wish to extend the party outdoors, the rear sliding glass doors open onto a deck. Back inside, the kitchen counter separating the work space from the family room hides the kitchen mess and doubles as an eating bar. On the second floor, three bedrooms all open onto a spectacular balcony, where a window seat is nested into the main dormer. This house is designed with basement, slab, and crawlspace foundation options. 🏛

Order on-line at www.familyhomeplans.com

top By removing the wall between the family room and living room, both spaces share in the views, light, and warming hearth.

above Lots of light from the breakfast nook's bay window floods the open kitchen and family room space. The raised counter provides space for informal eating.

left With glass doors front and back, the upper cabinets above the L-shaped kitchen island let light into the kitchen rather than blocking its flow.

right One of the home's most spectacular viewing points and one of its coziest getaway spots is this upper-level window seat set into the dormer that holds the tall round-top window.

below left A large forward-facing window in the master bedroom looks out onto the valley beyond. Just outside the bedroom is the round-top window and window seat shown above.

below right Although modifications made it a bit smaller, the master bath is still plenty accommodating thanks to a large whirlpool tub and clever storage solutions.

above The pleasing rectangular shape of the home, efficient and cost-effective to build, is clear from the rear view, which also shows the breakfast nook bay and one side of the wraparound porch.

Please note: The photographed home may have been modified to suit homeowner preferences. If you order plans, you may wish to have a builder or design professional check them against the photographs to confirm construction details.

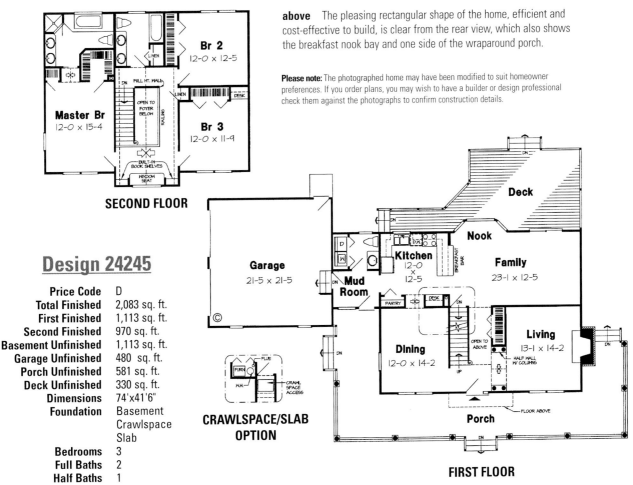

SECOND FLOOR

Master Br
12-0 x 15-4

Br 2
12-0 x 12-5

Br 3
12-0 x 11-9

Design 24245

Price Code	D
Total Finished	2,083 sq. ft.
First Finished	1,113 sq. ft.
Second Finished	970 sq. ft.
Basement Unfinished	1,113 sq. ft.
Garage Unfinished	480 sq. ft.
Porch Unfinished	581 sq. ft.
Deck Unfinished	330 sq. ft.
Dimensions	74'x41'6"
Foundation	Basement Crawlspace Slab
Bedrooms	3
Full Baths	2
Half Baths	1

CRAWLSPACE/SLAB OPTION

Garage
21-5 x 21-5

Mud Room

Kitchen
12-0 x 12-5

Nook

Family
23-1 x 12-5

Deck

Dining
12-0 x 14-2

Living
13-1 x 14-2

Porch

FIRST FLOOR

PHOTOGRAPHY: BOBBY AND WANDA CARROLL

Modifications MAKE IT RIGHT

Bobby Carroll knew what he wanted from retirement and it wasn't sitting on the porch and watching the world go by. It wasn't even really retirement at all. When he left Chevron Oil after many years, he and his wife, Wanda, moved to Tennessee, where Bobby picked up a hammer and did something that had interested him since childhood: He became a licensed contractor.

After working with a contractor friend for about six months, Bobby set out on his own. He says he built more than 20 houses in the five years he plied his new trade, before eventually deciding to really retire. Along the way, he had picked up the skills he needed to do something else he'd wanted to do for a long time, which was to build himself and his wife their own dream home, on their own perfect lot, back home in Texas.

The couple moved back to the Lone Star state, moved into an apartment, and began their search for the perfect lot and the perfect home plan.

They eventually found the perfect lot, which, by "no accident… was just steps away from the first fairway on the nearby golf course," says Bobby, an avid golfer who plays every day. All they needed now was the perfect plan. For that, they turned to a source they knew they could trust, a source with a huge selection of popular plans backed by a team of in-house experts, in-home design and customer service: The Garlinghouse Company.

When the Carrolls found their plan (number 92649), it was already fairly close to what they

above Stacked front-facing gables, a low, sheltering roof line, and a recessed covered entry present a traditionally welcoming facade to the street.

below Modifications to the great room included extending the length of the room, which allowed the addition of extra windows and a door to access a rear screen porch. A large screen TV took the place of the hearth.

left In the modified plan, the dining bay is aligned with the kitchen in one large open space. Eliminating the stairs not only allowed Bobby and Wanda to increase the size of the great room, they were also able to add an arched doorway providing direct access from the great room to the kitchen.

wanted. Bobby knew from experience, however, that a modification or two can turn a good stock home plan into the perfect custom home. Such modifications are usually slight, but they serve to customize a home to individual needs. And while Bobby knew that his professional experience would serve him well, he also knew that if he had any questions, he could turn to the Garlinghouse Design Team for help.

First, Bobby reversed the plan to better fit the lot, then he increased the footprint of the house on both ends, "a foot on the left and a foot on the right." That gave him and Wanda a bigger master bedroom and master bath and it freed space elsewhere in the house for a few other changes he had in mind.

At the same time he expanded the house laterally, he also increased the garage by one foot to the left and one foot toward the street. And because he chose the slab foundation over the basement foundation, he could take advantage of the space where the stairway would have been to increase the size of the great room from 16 feet 6 inches by 17 feet to 24 feet by 17 feet. He also eliminated the fireplace and replaced it with a "big screen high-definition television," the modern equivalent of the fireplace.

By increasing the great room, he moved the dining bay and the kitchen together into one large space, which eliminated the small porch in the corner between the original L-shape kitchen/dining area. Instead of the small porch, he added a large porch, 7 feet by 22 feet, which runs nearly the full length of the great room out back. They also took out a foot of the front porch and gave that over to the laundry room.

The Original Plan — #92649

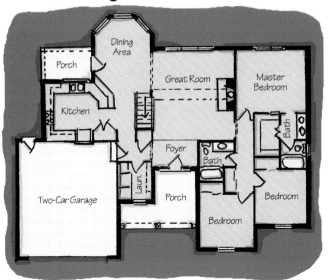

Carroll Residence

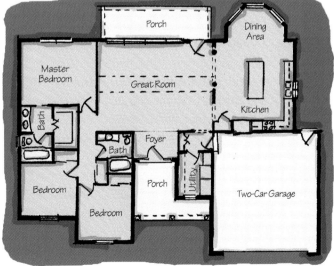

above & right The original plan as available for purchase.

Design 92649

Price Code	B
Total Finished	1,508 sq. ft.
Main Finished	1,508 sq. ft.
Basement Unfinished	1,439 sq. ft.
Garage Unfinished	440 sq. ft.
Dimensions	60'x47'
Foundation	Basement
Bedrooms	3
Full Baths	2

Please note: The photographed home was modified to suit homeowner preferences. If you order plans, you may wish to have a builder or design professional check them against the photographs to confirm construction details.

MAIN FLOOR

Smaller changes inside included the creation of arched openings between the main spaces, which Bobby personally built. "I knew what I wanted and I wanted to make sure I got just that," he said. And increasing the size of the garage gave the couple a 12 foot by 22 foot bonus area above the garage, giving them 264 square feet of storage space, which is accessed by a "big, heavy-duty, pull-down staircase."

Today Bobby and Wanda Carroll couldn't be happier with their new home and the decisions they made in customizing it. Both will testify that a few careful modifications can turn the almost perfect plan into the ideal custom home.

As a builder and homeowner, Bobby does advise caution when choosing a contractor, a profession that doesn't require a license in some states. That's not to say you shouldn't use an unlicensed professional, it just means that you should be extra careful in your search by checking references and seeing examples of recent work.

It's also very important that you find a company you can trust to help you decide on modifications, a company with people like the design team at Garlinghouse.

So if you think building your dream home is nothing but a pipe dream, look at Bobby and Wanda Carroll and think again. At Garlinghouse, we are here to help you build that dream, and we've been doing it for people like the Carrolls—and you—since 1907. 🏛

Design 32018

See Order Pages and Index for Info

REAR ELEVATION

PHOTOGRAPHY: COURTESY OF THE DESIGNER

Please note: The photographed home may have been modified to suit homeowner preferences. If you order plans, have a builder or design professional check them against the photograph to confirm actual construction details.

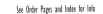

MAIN FLOOR

Units	Single
Price Code	A
Total Finished	663 sq. ft.
Main Finished	663 sq. ft.
Porch Unfinished	206 sq. ft.
Dimensions	23'6"x41'2"
Foundation	Pier/Post
Bedrooms	1
Full Baths	1
Main Ceiling	8'
Max Ridge Height	32'
Roof Framing	Stick
Exterior Walls	2x4

Design 19984

See Order Pages and Index for Info

Units	Single
Price Code	A
Total Finished	982 sq. ft.
Main Finished	982 sq. ft.
Garage Unfinished	208 sq. ft.
Dimensions	28'x51'4"
Foundation	Slab
Bedrooms	2
Full Baths	2
Main Ceiling	9'6"-8"
Max Ridge Height	15'
Roof Framing	Stick
Exterior Walls	2x6

PHOTOGRAPHY: COURTESY OF THE DESIGNER

Please note: The photographed home may have been modified to suit homeowner preferences. If you order plans, have a builder or design professional check them against the photograph to confirm actual construction details.

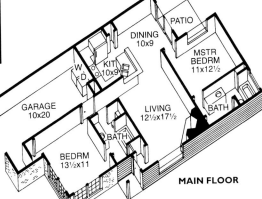

MAIN FLOOR

See thousands more plans at www.familyhomeplans.com

Design 65162

See Order Pages and Index for Info

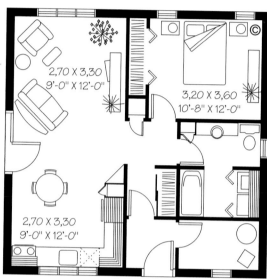

2,70 X 3,30
9'-0" X 12'-0"

3,20 X 3,60
10'-8" X 12'-0"

2,70 X 3,30
9'-0" X 12'-0"

MAIN FLOOR

Units	Single
Price Code	A
Total Finished	784 sq. ft.
Main Finished	784 sq. ft.
Dimensions	28'x28'
Foundation	Slab
Bedrooms	1
Full Baths	1
Main Ceiling	8'
Max Ridge Height	18'
Roof Framing	Truss

Design 90934

See Order Pages and Index for Info

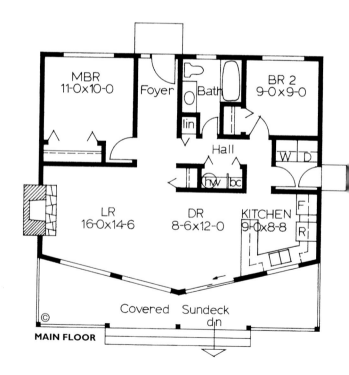

MBR
11-0x10-0

Foyer

Bath

BR 2
9-0x9-0

lin

Hall

W D

hw bc

LR
16-0x14-6

DR
8-6x12-0

KITCHEN
9-0x8-8

F
R

Covered   Sundeck
dn

MAIN FLOOR

Units	Single
Price Code	A
Total Finished	884 sq. ft.
Main Finished	884 sq. ft.
Deck Unfinished	170 sq. ft.
Dimensions	34'x31'
Foundation	Crawlspace
Bedrooms	2
Full Baths	1
Main Ceiling	8'
Max Ridge Height	15'6"
Roof Framing	Truss
Exterior Walls	2x6

Design 94307

See Order Pages and Index for Info

Units	Single
Price Code	A
Total Finished	786 sq. ft.
Main Finished	786 sq. ft.
Deck Unfinished	580 sq. ft.
Dimensions	46'x22'
Foundation	Crawlspace
Bedrooms	2
3/4 Baths	2
Main Ceiling	8'
Vaulted Ceiling	16'
Max Ridge Height	18'6"
Roof Framing	Truss
Exterior Walls	2x6

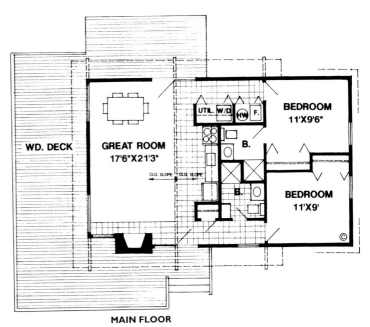

MAIN FLOOR

Design 65263

See Order Pages and Index for Info

Units	Single
Price Code	A
Total Finished	840 sq. ft.
Main Finished	840 sq. ft.
Porch Unfinished	466 sq. ft.
Dimensions	33'x31'
Foundation	Basement
Bedrooms	1
Full Baths	1
Main Ceiling	8'
Max Ridge Height	22'11"
Roof Framing	Truss
Exterior Walls	2x6

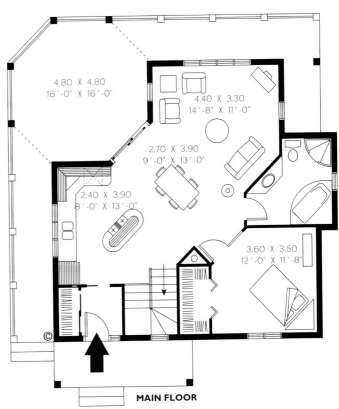

MAIN FLOOR

See thousands more plans at www.familyhomeplans.com

Design 10220

See Order Pages and Index for Info

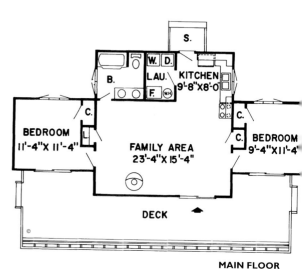

MAIN FLOOR

Units	Single
Price Code	A
Total Finished	888 sq. ft.
Main Finished	888 sq. ft.
Dimensions	50'x24'
Foundation	Slab
Bedrooms	2
Full Baths	1

Design 65018

Units	Single
Price Code	B
Total Finished	1,532 sq. ft.
First Finished	1,532 sq. ft.
Garage Unfinished	550 sq. ft.
Dimensions	59'x48'
Foundation	Basement
Bedrooms	3
Full Baths	1

FIRST FLOOR

Design 65642

See Order Pages and Index for Info

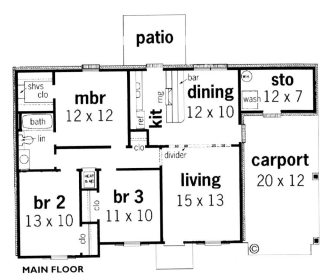

Units	Single
Price Code	A
Total Finished	998 sq. ft.
Main Finished	998 sq. ft.
Dimensions	48'x29'
Foundation	Crawlspace
	Slab
Bedrooms	3
Full Baths	1
Main Ceiling	8'
Max Ridge Height	26'
Roof Framing	Stick
Exterior Walls	2x4

Design 61093

See Order Pages and Index for Info

Units	Single
Price Code	A
Total Finished	930 sq. ft.
Main Finished	930 sq. ft.
Porch Unfinished	102 sq. ft.
Dimensions	35'x28'6"
Foundation	Crawlspace
	Slab
Bedrooms	3
Full Baths	1
Main Ceiling	8'
Roof Framing	Stick
Exterior Walls	2x4

See thousands more plans at www.familyhomeplans.com

Design 69030

See Order Pages and Index for Info

Units	Single
Price Code	A
Total Finished	914 sq. ft.
Main Finished	914 sq. ft.
Dimensions	28'x28'
Foundation	Basement
Bedrooms	2
Full Baths	1

Br 2
11-0x9-7

Kit
11-0x8-0

Deck

Dn

Dining

Dn

MBr
11-0x12-0

Living
12-7x19-4

Porch depth 5-0

MAIN FLOOR

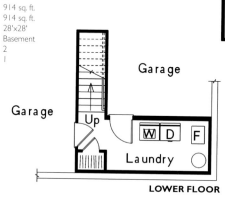

Garage

Garage

Up

W D F

Laundry

LOWER FLOOR

Design 65006

See Order Pages and Index for Info

Units	Single
Price Code	A
Total Finished	920 sq. ft.
Main Finished	920 sq. ft.
Porch Unfinished	152 sq. ft.
Dimensions	38'x28'
Foundation	Basement
Bedrooms	2
Full Baths	1
Main Ceiling	8'
Max Ridge Height	20'6"
Roof Framing	Truss
Exterior Walls	2x6

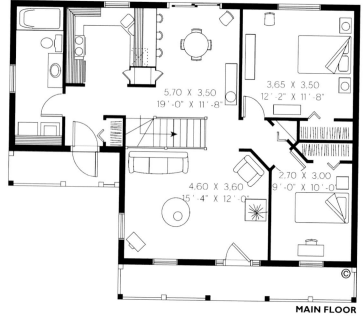

5.70 X 3.50
19'-0" X 11'-8"

3.65 X 3.50
12'-2" X 11'-8"

4.60 X 3.60
15'-4" X 12'-0"

2.70 X 3.00
9'-0" X 10'-0"

MAIN FLOOR

Design 51004

See Order Pages and Index for Info

Units	Single
Price Code	A
Total Finished	936 sq. ft.
Main Finished	936 sq. ft.
Basement Unfinished	936 sq. ft.
Porch Unfinished	42 sq. ft.
Dimensions	32'x34'8"
Foundation	Basement
Bedrooms	2
Full Baths	1
Main Ceiling	8'
Max Ridge Height	19'
Roof Framing	Truss
Exterior Walls	2x4

BR. #1
11/5X12/5

DINING
8/0X11/5

KIT
8/8X11/5

LIVING
19/9X13/9
VLTD' CLG.

BR. #2
11/5X10/10

DN

MAIN FLOOR

Design 55014

See Order Pages and Index for Info

Units	Single
Price Code	A
Total Finished	988 sq. ft.
Main Finished	988 sq. ft.
Dimensions	38'x32'
Foundation	Basement
Bedrooms	3
Full Baths	1
Main Ceiling	9'
Max Ridge Height	20'
Roof Framing	Truss

br2
9'x9'

br3
9'x9'

VAULTED
din
8'x9'4

VAULTED
k
7'6x9'

VAULTED
liv
15'x15'8

mbr
13'x12'4

RAILING

D
W

PORCH

See thousands more plans at www.familyhomeplans.com

Design 65387

See Order Pages and Index for Info

Units	Single
Price Code	A
Total Finished	948 sq. ft.
Main Finished	948 sq. ft.
Dimensions	30'x34'
Foundation	Basement
Bedrooms	2
Full Baths	1
Roof Framing	Stick

FRONT ELEVATION

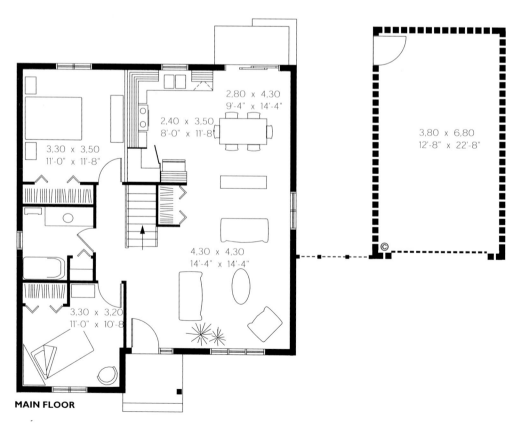

2,80 x 4,30
9'-4" x 14'-4"

2,40 x 3,50
8'-0" x 11'-8"

3,30 x 3,50
11'-0" x 11'-8"

3,80 x 6,80
12'-8" x 22'-8"

4,30 x 4,30
14'-4" x 14'-4"

3,30 x 3,20
11'-0" x 10'-8

MAIN FLOOR

Design 65026

See Order Pages and Index for Info

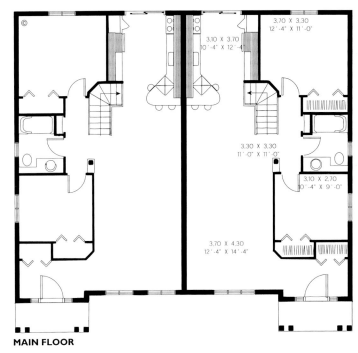

Units	Duplex
Price Code	C
Total Finished	946 sq. ft. per unit
Main Finished	946 sq. ft. per unit
Dimensions	48'x40'
Foundation	Basement
Bedrooms	2 per unit
Full Baths	1 per unit

3.70 X 3.30
12'-4" X 11'-0"

3.10 X 3.70
10'-4" X 12'-4"

3.30 X 3.30
11'-0" X 11'-0"

3.10 X 2.70
10'-4" X 9'-0"

3.70 X 4.30
12'-4" X 14'-4"

MAIN FLOOR

Design 65005

See Order Pages and Index for Info

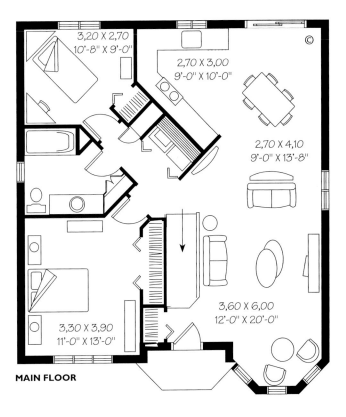

Units	Single
Price Code	A
Total Finished	972 sq. ft.
Main Finished	972 sq. ft.
Basement Unfinished	972 sq. ft.
Dimensions	30'x35'
Foundation	Basement
Bedrooms	2
Full Baths	1
Main Ceiling	8'2"
Max Ridge Height	17'6"
Exterior Walls	2x6

3.20 X 2.70
10'-8" X 9'-0"

2.70 X 3.00
9'-0" X 10'-0"

2.70 X 4.10
9'-0" X 13'-8"

3.60 X 6.00
12'-0" X 20'-0"

3.30 X 3.90
11'-0" X 13'-0"

MAIN FLOOR

Design 65003

See Order Pages and Index for Info

Units	Single
Price Code	A
Total Finished	976 sq. ft.
First Finished	593 sq. ft.
Second Finished	383 sq. ft.
Basement Unfinished	593 sq. ft.
Dimensions	22'8"x26'8"
Foundation	Crawlspace
Bedrooms	2
Full Baths	1
3/4 Baths	1
First Ceiling	8'
Second Ceiling	8'
Max Ridge Height	22'8"
Roof Framing	Truss
Exterior Walls	2x6

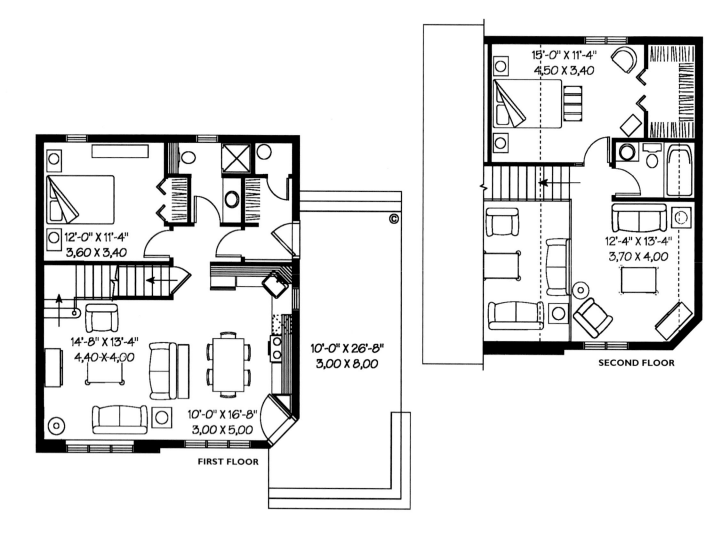

15'-0" X 11'-4"
4.50 X 3.40

12'-4" X 13'-4"
3.70 X 4.00

SECOND FLOOR

12'-0" X 11'-4"
3.60 X 3.40

14'-8" X 13'-4"
4.40 X 4.00

10'-0" X 26'-8"
3.00 X 8.00

10'-0" X 16'-8"
3.00 X 5.00

FIRST FLOOR

Design 24302

See Order Pages and Index for Info

PHOTOGRAPHY: COURTESY OF THE DESIGNER

Units	Single
Price Code	A
Total Finished	988 sq. ft.
Main Finished	988 sq. ft.
Basement Unfinished	988 sq. ft.
Garage Unfinished	280 sq. ft.
Dimensions	54'x28'
Foundation	Basement
	Crawlspace
Bedrooms	3
Full Baths	1
3/4 Baths	1
Main Ceiling	8'
Max Ridge Height	18'
Roof Framing	Stick
Exterior Walls	2x4

Please note: The photographed home may have been modified to suit homeowner preferences. If you order plans, have a builder or design professional check them against the photograph to confirm actual construction details.

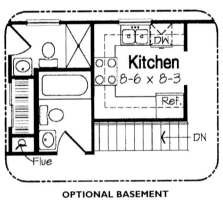

**OPTIONAL BASEMENT
STAIR LOCATION**

FRONT ELEVATION

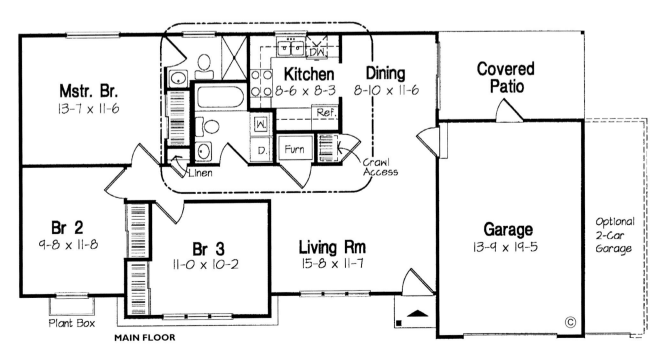

MAIN FLOOR

Design 65033

See Order Pages and Index for Info

MAIN FLOOR

Units	Single
Price Code	A
Total Finished	994 sq. ft.
Main Finished	994 sq. ft.
Basement Unfinished	994 sq. ft.
Dimensions	38'x32'
Foundation	Basement
Bedrooms	2
Full Baths	1
Main Ceiling	8'
Max Ridge Height	18'6"
Roof Framing	Truss
Exterior Walls	2x6

Design 92426

See Order Pages and Index for Info

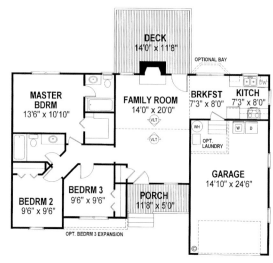

Units	Single
Price Code	A
Total Finished	997 sq. ft.
Main Finished	997 sq. ft.
Dimensions	49'6"x33'6"
Foundation	Crawlspace
Bedrooms	3
Full Baths	2
Max Ridge Height	16'
Roof Framing	Stick
Exterior Walls	2x4

Design 65011

See Order Pages and Index for Info

Units	Single
Price Code	A
Total Finished	996 sq. ft.
First Finished	100 sq. ft.
Second Finished	896 sq. ft.
Garage Unfinished	796 sq. ft.
Dimensions	28'×32'
Foundation	Slab
Bedrooms	2
3/4 Baths	1
Half Baths	1
Main Ceiling	8'2"
Max Ridge Height	26'10"
Roof Framing	Truss
Exterior Walls	2x6

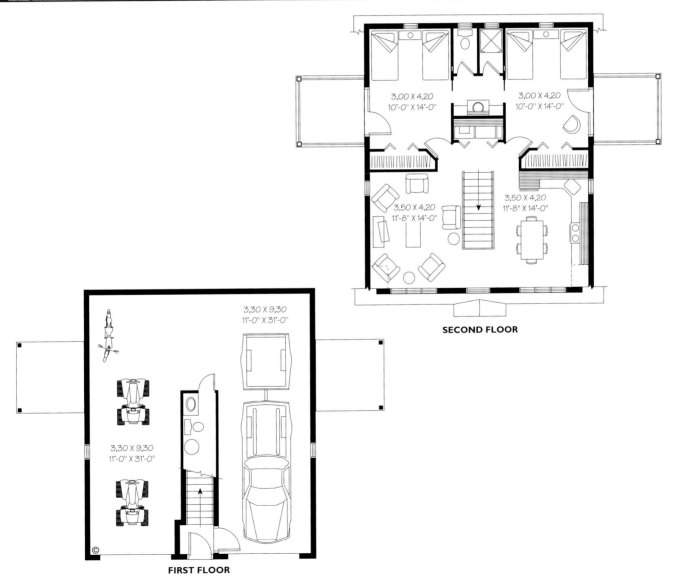

SECOND FLOOR

FIRST FLOOR

Design 65140

See Order Pages and Index for Info

Units	Single
Price Code	A
Total Finished	1,258 sq. ft.
First Finished	753 sq. ft.
Second Finished	505 sq. ft.
Basement Unfinished	753 sq. ft.
Dimensions	30'×28'
Foundation	Basement
Bedrooms	3
Full Baths	1
Half Baths	1
First Ceiling	8'
Second Ceiling	8'
Max Ridge Height	24'10"
Roof Framing	Truss
Exterior Walls	2x6

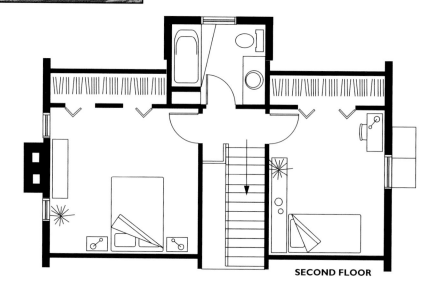

SECOND FLOOR

3,70 x 3,40
12'-4" x 11'-4"

3,20 x 2,60
10'-8" x 8'-8"

4,50 x 3,70
15'-0" x 12'-4"

3,00 x 2,70
10'-0" x 9'-0"

FIRST FLOOR

Design 65284

See Order Pages and Index for Info

Units	Single
Price Code	A
Total Finished	1,324 sq. ft.
First Finished	737 sq. ft.
Second Finished	587 sq. ft.
Dimensions	26'×33'
Foundation	Basement
Bedrooms	1 or 2
Full Baths	1
Half Baths	1
First Ceiling	8'
Second Ceiling	8'
Max Ridge Height	34'9"
Roof Framing	Truss
Exterior Walls	2x6

**OPTIONAL SECOND FLOOR
WITH TWO BEDROOMS**

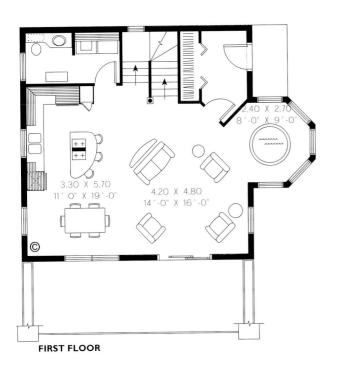

FIRST FLOOR

**OPTIONAL SECOND FLOOR
WITH ONE BEDROOM**

Design 65173

See Order Pages and Index for Info

Units	Single
Price Code	A
Total Finished	1,311 sq. ft.
First Finished	713 sq. ft.
Second Finished	598 sq. ft.
Basement Unfinished	713 sq. ft.
Porch Unfinished	158 sq. ft.
Dimensions	30'8"×26'
Foundation	Basement
Bedrooms	2
Full Baths	1
3/4 Baths	1
First Ceiling	8'
Second Ceiling	8'
Max Ridge Height	28'4"
Roof Framing	Truss
Exterior Walls	2x6

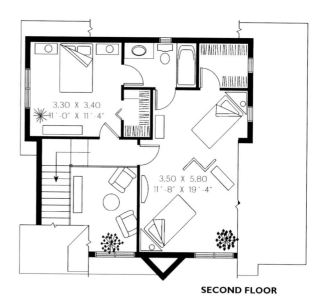

SECOND FLOOR

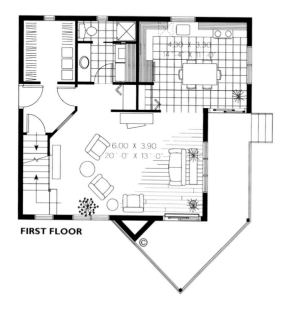

FIRST FLOOR

Design 65014

See Order Pages and Index for Info

Units	Single
Price Code	A
Total Finished	1,148 sq. ft.
First Finished	728 sq. ft.
Second Finished	420 sq. ft.
Bonus Unfinished	728 sq. ft.
Porch Unfinished	187 sq. ft.
Dimensions	28'x26'
Foundation	Basement
Bedrooms	1
Full Baths	1
Half Baths	1
First Ceiling	8'
Second Ceiling	8'
Max Ridge Height	25'4"
Exterior Walls	2x6

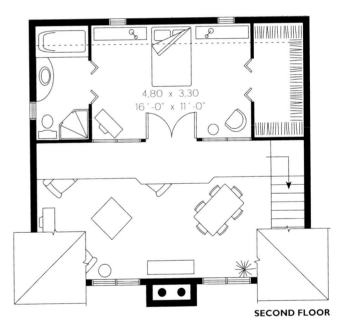

SECOND FLOOR

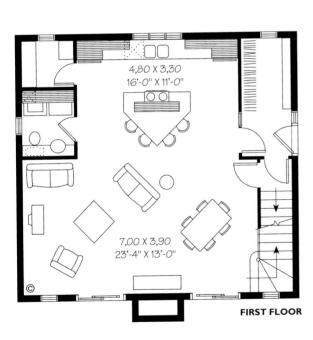

4,80 X 3,30
16'-0" X 11'-0"

7,00 X 3,90
23'-4" X 13'-0"

FIRST FLOOR

See thousands more plans at www.familyhomeplans.com

Design 65242

See Order Pages and Index for Info

Units	Single
Price Code	A
Total Finished	1,152 sq. ft.
First Finished	576 sq. ft.
Second Finished	576 sq. ft.
Dimensions	24'x24'
Foundation	Basement
Bedrooms	3
Full Baths	1
Half Baths	1

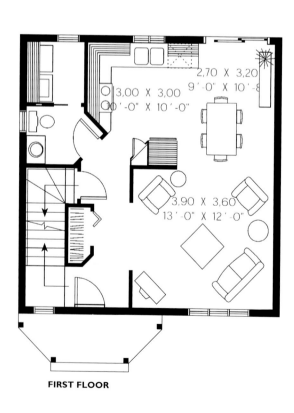

2,70 X 3,20
9'-0" X 10'-8

3,00 X 3,00
'-0" X 10'-0"

3,90 X 3,60
13'-0" X 12'-0"

FIRST FLOOR

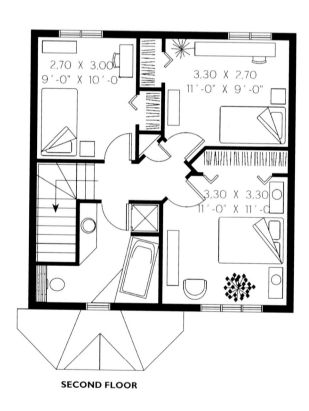

2,70 X 3,00
9'-0" X 10'-0"

3,30 X 2,70
11'-0" X 9'-0"

3,30 X 3,30
11'-0" X 11'-0"

SECOND FLOOR

Design 32323

See Order Pages and Index for Info

PHOTOGRAPHY: ED GOHLICH

LIVING ROOM/KITCHEN

Please note: The photographed home may have been modified to suit homeowner preferences. If you order plans, have a builder or design professional check them against the photograph to confirm actual construction details.

Units	Single
Price Code	A
Total Finished	1,200 sq. ft.
Main Finished	1,200 sq. ft.
Porch Unfinished	200 sq. ft.
Dimensions	51'4"x34'
Foundation	Crawlspace
Bedrooms	2
Full Baths	2
Main Ceiling	8'
Vaulted Ceiling	12'4"
Max Ridge Height	16'4"
Roof Framing	Stick
Exterior Walls	2x4

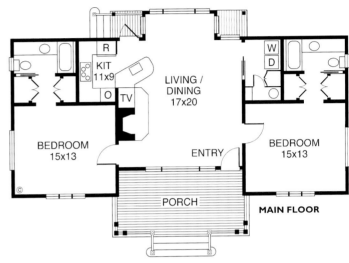

MAIN FLOOR

Design 32192

See Order Pages and Index for Info

PHOTOGRAPHY: JAMES SALOMON

Units	Single
Price Code	A
Total Finished	1,214 sq. ft.
First Finished	1,114 sq. ft.
Second Finished	100 sq. ft.
Deck Unfinished	441 sq. ft.
Porch Unfinished	120 sq. ft.
Dimensions	48'4"x47'
Foundation	Crawlspace
Bedrooms	3
Full Baths	1
Vaulted Ceiling	17'
Max Ridge Height	20'4"
Roof Framing	Stick
Exterior Walls	2x6

Please note: The photographed home may have been modified to suit homeowner preferences. If you order plans, have a builder or design professional check them against the photograph to confirm actual construction details.

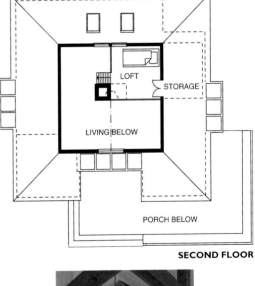

SECOND FLOOR

FIRST FLOOR

LIVING ROOM

Design **90048**

See Order Pages and Index for Info

Units	Single
Price Code	A
Total Finished	1,274 sq. ft.
First Finished	974 sq. ft.
Second Finished	300 sq. ft.
Basement Unfinished	974 sq. ft.
Dimensions	23'8"x55'10"
Foundation	Basement
Bedrooms	3
Full Baths	2
Max Ridge Height	23'
Roof Framing	Stick
Exterior Walls	2x4

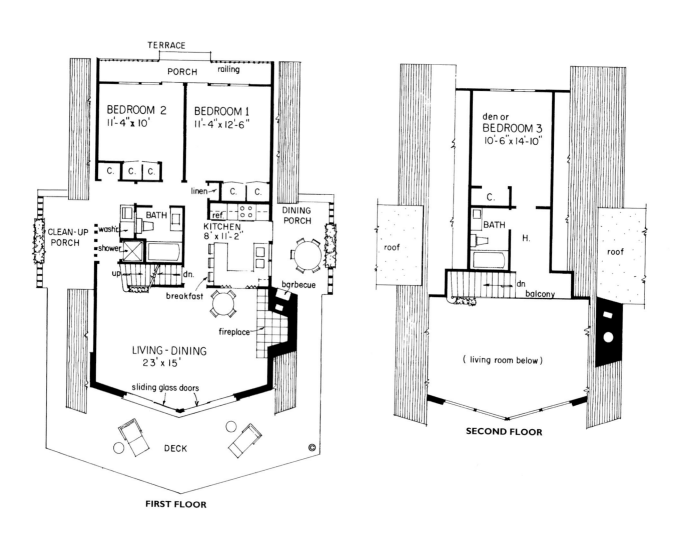

FIRST FLOOR

SECOND FLOOR

Design 20161

See Order Pages and Index for Info

Units	Single
Price Code	A
Total Finished	1,307 sq. ft.
Main Finished	1,307 sq. ft.
Basement Unfinished	1,298 sq. ft.
Garage Unfinished	462 sq. ft.
Dimensions	50'x40'
Foundation	Basement
	Crawlspace
	Slab
Bedrooms	3
Full Baths	2
Main Ceiling	8'
Max Ridge Height	19'
Roof Framing	Stick
Exterior Walls	2x6

PHOTOGRAPHY: JOHN EHRENCLOU

REAR ELEVATION

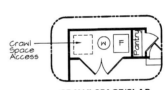

**CRAWLSPACE/SLAB
FOUNDATION OPTION**

Please note: The photographed home may have been modified to suit homeowner preferences. If you order plans, have a builder or design professional check them against the photograph to confirm actual construction details.

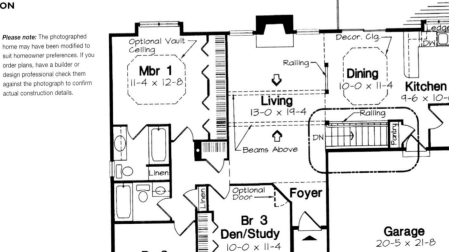

MAIN FLOOR

Design 52015

See Order Pages and Index for Info

Units	Single
Price Code	A
Total Finished	1,304 sq. ft.
Main Finished	1,304 sq. ft.
Basement Unfinished	1,326 sq. ft.
Garage Unfinished	458 sq. ft.
Dimensions	50'x41'
Foundation	Basement
	Crawlspace
Bedrooms	3
Full Baths	2
Main Ceiling	8'
Max Ridge Height	23'6'
Roof Framing	Stick
Exterior Walls	2x4

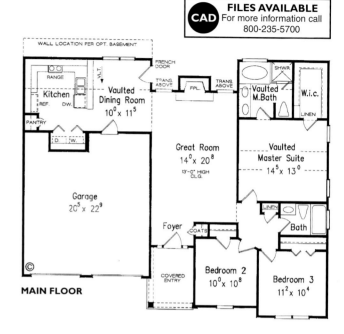

MAIN FLOOR

OPTIONAL BASEMENT STAIR LOCATION

Design 34600

See Order Pages and Index for Info

PHOTOGRAPHY: MICHELE EVANS CHRISTY

REAR ELEVATION

CRAWLSPACE/SLAB FOUNDATION OPTION

Units	Single
Price Code	A
Total Finished	1,328 sq. ft.
First Finished	1,013 sq. ft.
Second Finished	315 sq. ft.
Basement Unfinished	1,013 sq. ft.
Dimensions	36'x36'
Foundation	Basement
	Crawlspace
	Slab
Bedrooms	3
Full Baths	2
First Ceiling	8'
Second Ceiling	7'6"
Max Ridge Height	23'6"
Roof Framing	Stick
Exterior Walls	2x4, 2x6

SECOND FLOOR

FIRST FLOOR

Please note: The photographed home may have been modified to suit homeowner preferences. If you order plans, have a builder or design professional check them against the photograph to confirm actual construction details.

Design 98434

See Order Pages and Index for Info

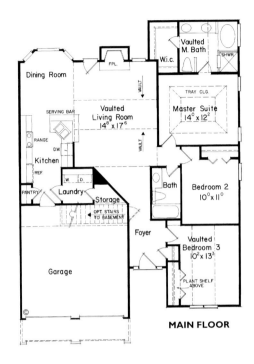

MAIN FLOOR

Units	Single
Price Code	A
Total Finished	1,346 sq. ft.
Main Finished	1,346 sq. ft.
Basement Unfinished	1,358 sq. ft.
Garage Unfinished	395 sq. ft.
Dimensions	39'x51'
Foundation	Basement
	Crawlspace
	Slab
Bedrooms	3
Full Baths	2
Max Ridge Height	21'6"
Roof Framing	Stick
Exterior Walls	2x4

Design 82003

See Order Pages and Index for Info

MAIN FLOOR

Units	Single
Price Code	A
Total Finished	1,379 sq. ft.
Main Finished	1,379 sq. ft.
Garage Unfinished	493 sq. ft.
Porch Unfinished	142 sq. ft.
Dimensions	38'4"x68'6"
Foundation	Crawlspace
	Slab
Bedrooms	3
Full Baths	2
Main Ceiling	9'
Roof Framing	Stick
Exterior Walls	2x4

See thousands more plans at www.familyhomeplans.com

Design 91026

See Order Pages and Index for Info

Units	Single
Price Code	A
Total Finished	1,354 sq. ft.
First Finished	988 sq. ft.
Second Finished	366 sq. ft.
Basement Unfinished	742 sq. ft.
Garage Unfinished	283 sq. ft.
Dimensions	26'x48'
Foundation	Basement
Bedrooms	3
Full Baths	1
3/4 Baths	1
First Ceiling	8'
Vaulted Ceiling	13'6"
Max Ridge Height	32'
Roof Framing	Stick
Exterior Walls	2x6

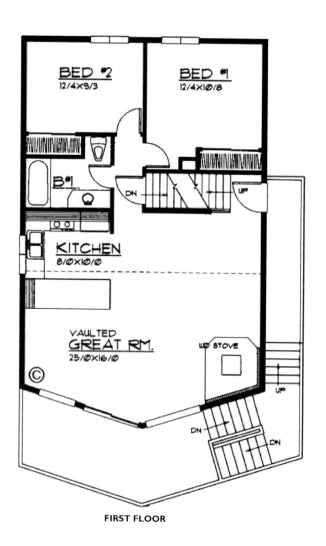

FIRST FLOOR

BED #2
12/4x9/3

BED #1
12/4x10/8

B #1

KITCHEN
8/0x10/0

VAULTED
GREAT RM.
25/0x16/0

UP STOVE

DN

DN

DN

UP

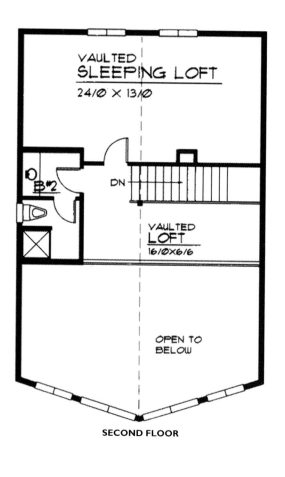

SECOND FLOOR

VAULTED
SLEEPING LOFT
24/0 X 13/0

B #2

DN

VAULTED
LOFT
16/0x6/6

OPEN TO
BELOW

1,000-1,500 Sq. Ft.

Design 20156

See Order Pages and Index for Info

PHOTOGRAPHY: COURTESY OF THE DESIGNER

REAR ELEVATION

Units	Single
Price Code	A
Total Finished	1,359 sq. ft.
Main Finished	1,359 sq. ft.
Basement Unfinished	1,359 sq. ft.
Garage Unfinished	501 sq. ft.
Dimensions	58'x34'4"
Foundation	Basement
	Crawlspace
	Slab
Bedrooms	3
Full Baths	2
Main Ceiling	8'
Max Ridge Height	18'6"
Roof Framing	Stick
Exterior Walls	2x4, 2x6

CRAWLSPACE/SLAB FOUNDATION OPTION

Please note: The photographed home may have been modified to suit homeowner preferences. If you order plans, have a builder or design professional check them against the photograph to confirm actual construction details.

Design 98411

See Order Pages and Index for Info

FILES AVAILABLE
For more information call
800-235-5700

Units	Single
Price Code	A
Total Finished	1,373 sq. ft.
Main Finished	1,373 sq. ft.
Basement Unfinished	1,386 sq. ft.
Dimensions	50'4"x45'
Foundation	Basement
	Crawlspace
Bedrooms	3
Full Baths	2
Main Ceiling	9'
Max Ridge Height	23'6"
Roof Framing	Stick
Exterior Walls	2x4, 2x6

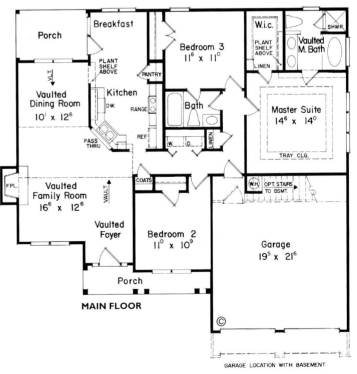

Design 65134

Units	Single
Price Code	A
Total Finished	1,304 sq. ft.
First Finished	681 sq. ft.
Second Finished	623 sq. ft.
Garage Unfinished	260 sq. ft.
Dimensions	28'x40'
Foundation	Basement
Bedrooms	2
Full Baths	1
Half Baths	1
First Ceiling	8'
Second Ceiling	8'
Roof Framing	Truss
Exterior Walls	2x6

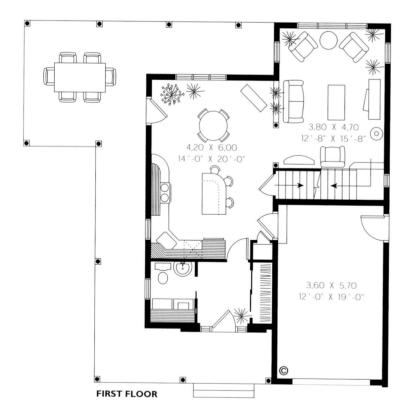

FIRST FLOOR

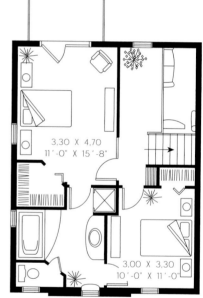

SECOND FLOOR

Design 34601

See Order Pages and Index for Info

Units	Single
Price Code	A
Total Finished	1,415 sq. ft.
First Finished	1,007 sq. ft.
Second Finished	408 sq. ft.
Basement Unfinished	1,007 sq. ft.
Porch Unfinished	300 sq. ft.
Dimensions	38'4"x36'
Foundation	Basement
	Crawlspace
	Slab
Bedrooms	3
Full Baths	2
First Ceiling	8'
Second Ceiling	8'
Max Ridge Height	24'6"
Roof Framing	Stick
Exterior Walls	2x4, 2x6

REAR ELEVATION

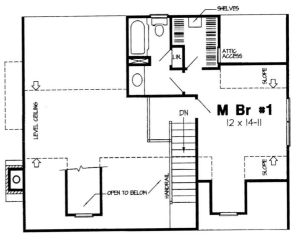

SECOND FLOOR

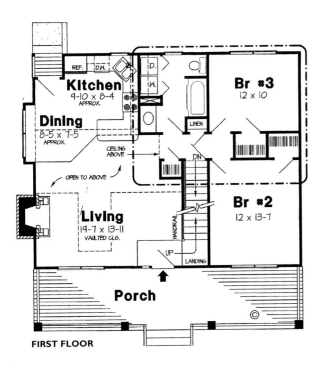

FIRST FLOOR

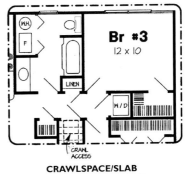

**CRAWLSPACE/SLAB
FOUNDATION OPTION**

Design 98415

See Order Pages and Index for Info

Units	Single
Price Code	A
Total Finished	1,429 sq. ft.
Main Finished	1,429 sq. ft.
Basement Unfinished	1,472 sq. ft.
Garage Unfinished	438 sq. ft.
Dimensions	49'x53'
Foundation	Basement
	Crawlspace
	Slab
Bedrooms	3
Full Baths	2
Main Ceiling	8'
Max Ridge Height	23'
Roof Framing	Stick
Exterior Walls	2x4

Master Suite 12⁰ x 15⁷ TRAY CLG.

Breakfast

Bedroom 3 11⁰ x 10²

Kitchen

RANGE

DW.

REF.

Vaulted Family Room 16² x 17⁵ 15'-3" HIGH CLG.

SERVING BAR

Bath

LIN.

FPL.

PLANT SHELF ABOVE

VAULT

Vaulted M.Bath

WET BAR

Foyer 12'-0" HIGH CLG.

Bedroom 2 11⁰ x 10¹

SHWR.

PLANT SHELF ABOVE

CTS.

W.

D.

Laun.

Dining Room 10¹ x 11¹⁰ 14'-0" HIGH CLG.

Covered Porch

W.i.c.

Storage

OPT. STAIRS TO BASEMENT

MAIN FLOOR

Garage 19⁵ x 19⁷

Design 97274

See Order Pages and Index for Info

Units	Single
Price Code	A
Total Finished	1,432 sq. ft.
Main Finished	1,432 sq. ft.
Basement Unfinished	1,454 sq. ft.
Garage Unfinished	440 sq. ft.
Dimensions	49'x52'4"
Foundation	Basement
	Crawlspace
Bedrooms	3
Full Baths	2
Max Ridge Height	24'2"
Roof Framing	Stick
Exterior Walls	2x4

TRAY CEILING

Breakfast

FRENCH DOOR

FPL.

Bedroom 3 11⁰ x 10²

Master Suite 12⁰ x 15⁷

RANGE

DW.

PASS-THRU

VAULT

Vaulted Great Room 16¹ x 17⁵ 15'-3" CLG. HT.

LINEN

Bath

FRENCH DOOR

Kitchen

REF.

PANTRY

Vaulted M.Bath

PLANT SHELF ABOVE

ARCHED OPENING

Foyer 12'-0" CLG. HT.

COATS

SHWR.

W.i.c.

LINEN

W.

D.

Laund.

Dining Room 11¹ x 12⁰ 12'-0" CLG. HT.

Bedroom 2 11⁰ x 10¹

OPT. STAIRS TO BSMT.

COVERED PORCH

MAIN FLOOR

Garage 19⁵ x 21⁹

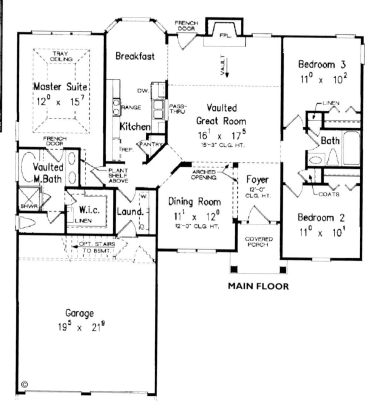

Design 24711

See Order Pages and Index for Info

Units	Single
Price Code	A
Total Finished	1,434 sq. ft.
First Finished	1,018 sq. ft.
Second Finished	416 sq. ft.
Basement Unfinished	1,008 sq. ft.
Garage Unfinished	624 sq. ft.
Porch Unfinished	288 sq. ft.
Dimensions	73'x36'
Foundation	Basement Crawlspace Slab
Bedrooms	3
Full Baths	2
Max Ridge Height	24'6"
Roof Framing	Stick
Exterior Walls	2x4

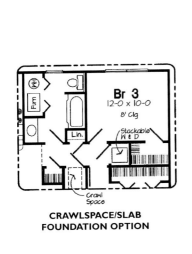

**CRAWLSPACE/SLAB
FOUNDATION OPTION**

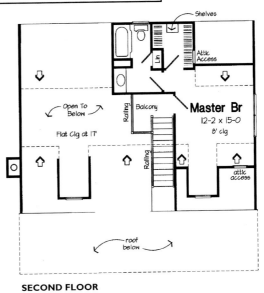

SECOND FLOOR

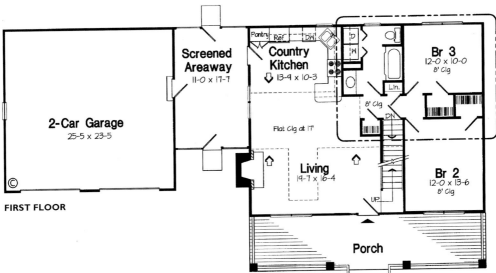

FIRST FLOOR

Design 96509

See Order Pages and Index for Info

Units	Single
Price Code	A
Total Finished	1,056 sq. ft.
First Finished	576 sq. ft.
Second Finished	480 sq. ft.
Basement Unfinished	576 sq. ft.
Deck Unfinished	315 sq. ft.
Porch Unfinished	45 sq. ft.
Dimensions	24'x30'
Foundation	Basement
Bedrooms	2
Full Baths	I
Half Baths	I
First Ceiling	8'
Second Ceiling	8'
Max Ridge Height	23'
Roof Framing	Truss
Exterior Walls	2x6

SECOND FLOOR

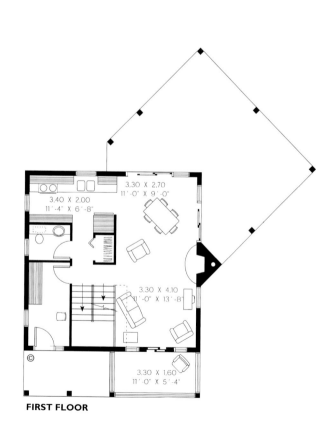

FIRST FLOOR

1,000-1,500 Sq. Ft.

Design 24706

See Order Pages and Index for Info

REAR ELEVATION

Please note: The photographed home may have been modified to suit homeowner preferences. If you order plans, have a builder or design professional check them against the photograph to confirm actual construction details.

PHOTOGRAPHY: COURTESY OF THE DESIGNER

Units	Single
Price Code	A
Total Finished	1,470 sq. ft.
First Finished	1,035 sq. ft.
Second Finished	435 sq. ft.
Basement Unfinished	1,018 sq. ft.
Deck Unfinished	240 sq. ft.
Porch Unfinished	192 sq. ft.
Dimensions	35'x42'
Foundation	Basement
	Crawlspace
	Slab
Bedrooms	3
Full Baths	2
First Ceiling	8'
Second Ceiling	8'
Max Ridge Height	27'
Roof Framing	Stick
Exterior Walls	2x4, 2x6

**CRAWLSPACE/SLAB
FOUNDATION OPTION**

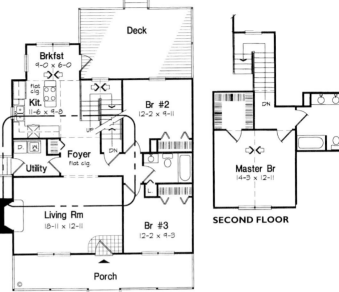

SECOND FLOOR

FIRST FLOOR

Design 65001

See Order Pages and Index for Info

Units	Single
Price Code	A
Total Finished	1,480 sq. ft.
First Finished	1,024 sq. ft.
Second Finished	456 sq. ft.
Basement Unfinished	1,024 sq. ft.
Dimensions	32'x40'
Foundation	Basement
Bedrooms	2
Full Baths	2
First Ceiling	8'
Second Ceiling	8'
Max Ridge Height	23'8"
Roof Framing	Truss
Exterior Walls	2x6

SECOND FLOOR

FIRST FLOOR

See thousands more plans at www.familyhomeplans.com

47

Design 34150

See Order Pages and Index for Info

PHOTOGRAPHY: JOHN EHRENCLOU

Units	Single
Price Code	A
Total Finished	1,492 sq. ft.
Main Finished	1,492 sq. ft.
Basement Unfinished	1,486 sq. ft.
Garage Unfinished	462 sq. ft.
Dimensions	56'x48'
Foundation	Basement Crawlspace Slab
Bedrooms	3
Full Baths	2
Main Ceiling	8'
Vaulted Ceiling	13'
Max Ridge Height	19'
Roof Framing	Stick
Exterior Walls	2x4, 2x6

Please note: The photographed home may have been modified to suit homeowner preferences. If you order plans, have a builder or design professional check them against the photograph to confirm actual construction details.

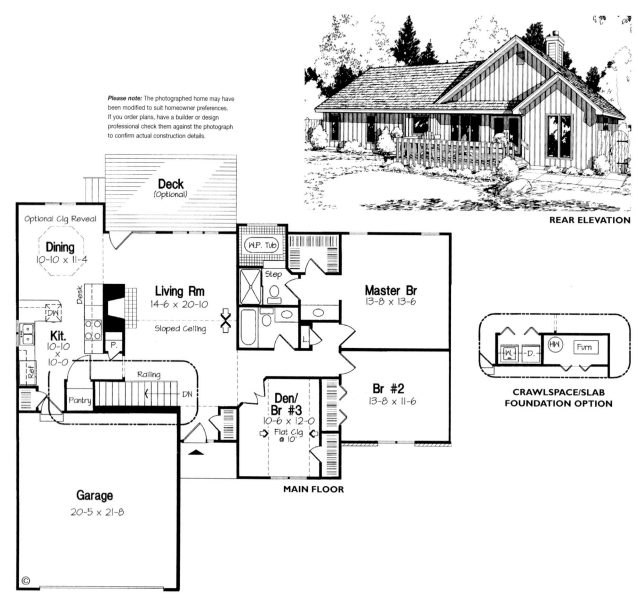

REAR ELEVATION

MAIN FLOOR

CRAWLSPACE/SLAB
FOUNDATION OPTION

above Perfect for a narrow lot, the garage on this home is tucked into the rear, which also prevents it from dominating the facade.

Please note: The photographed home may have been modified to suit homeowner preferences. If you order plans, you may wish to have a builder or design professional check them against the photographs to confirm construction details.

Design 82020

Price Code	C
Total Finished	1,845 sq. ft.
Main Finished	1,845 sq. ft.
Bonus Unfinished	1,191 sq. ft.
Garage Unfinished	496 sq. ft.
Porch Unfinished	465 sq. ft.
Dimensions	41'4"x83'8"
Foundation	Crawlspace Slab
Bedrooms	3
Full Baths	2

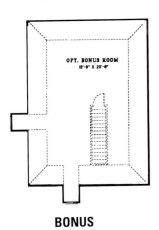

BONUS

MAIN FLOOR

family SPACES

The porch opens directly into the great room, which features a gas fireplace. To the right of the entrance, a short hallway connects the two secondary bedrooms to a full bath. Past the great room is the dining room and large kitchen/breakfast area. The kitchen, almost completely enveloped by counter space, holds a snack bar and built-in computer center. Off the breakfast room, a kid's nook features a bench with storage and sits near a laundry room. The breakfast nook has access to the grilling porch. The master suite features ample closet space and a luxurious whirlpool tub. This home is designed with slab and crawlspace foundation options. 🏛

PHOTOGRAPHY: JAMES YOCHUM

farmhouse FAVORITE

above   A center gable topping the covered porch promotes a sense of balance.

below   The big master suite at the rear of the home features three closets.

All the right spaces in all the right places are packed into this efficient beauty, including formal and informal living spaces as well as three bedrooms—all in just 1,550 square feet. A simple footprint makes the design extremely cost-efficient to build. The front porch (not shown on the floor plan) lines the living room, which feels even more spacious because it opens to the dining room. The U-shape kitchen maximizes space and seems larger than it is because it opens into the breakfast area and den, which can include a fireplace. A laundry area, closet and powder room complete the 775-square-foot first floor. On the second floor, double doors open to the master suite. This home is designed with a basement foundation. 🏛

Design 32229

Price Code	B
Total Finished	1,550 sq. ft.
First Finished	775 sq. ft.
Second Finished	775 sq. ft.
Basement Unfinished	775 sq. ft.
Deck Unfinished	112 sq. ft.
Porch Unfinished	150 sq. ft.
Dimensions	25'x37'
Foundation	Basement
Bedrooms	3
Full Baths	1
3/4 Baths	1
Half Baths	1

above As part of an open floor plan, the living room offers an elegant and unrestricted area for entertaining.

above left Windows lining the kitchen sink brighten up the room.

Please note: The photographed home may have been modified to suit homeowner preferences. If you order plans, you may wish to have a builder or design professional check them against the photographs to confirm construction details.

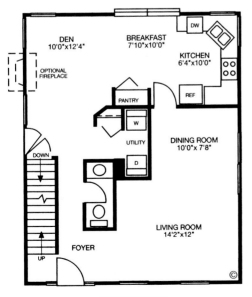

FIRST FLOOR

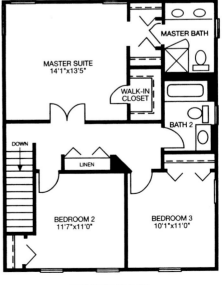

SECOND FLOOR

See thousands more plans at www.familyhomeplans.com

PHOTOGRAPHY: JAY GRAHAM

snug FIT

above & below   Designing a home to be built within setbacks on a tight lot doesn't mean sacrificing style.

Please note: The photographed home may have been modified to suit homeowner preferences. If you order plans, you may wish to have a builder or design professional check them against the photographs to confirm construction details.

Designed to take advantage of every inch of a small site, this plan achieves an open—even soaring—look with loads of style. The exterior is wrapped in richly textured shingle siding mixed with board-and-batten siding, which is common for bungalows and cottages. Not as common are the home's open spaces and light—filled rooms, not to mention its subtle nautical theme-from the living room fireplace built with boatlike angles to the crow's nest of a tower that houses an office. The living room and family room sit just off the entryway, with the dining room conveniently located next to the space-efficient kitchen. The 647-square-foot second floor is given over to the master suite and complementary private spaces, which include a sleeping porch and private deck. There are 877 square feet on the first floor. This home is designed with a crawlspace foundation. 🏛

SMART DESIGNS for smaller lots

above   The homeowner modified the plan to include a compact home office set into the soaring light tower.

above left   The board-and-batten chimney provides the living room with an appropriately nautical feel thanks to its boat-like angles.

left   Triple windows help brighten the already well-lit vaulted living room.

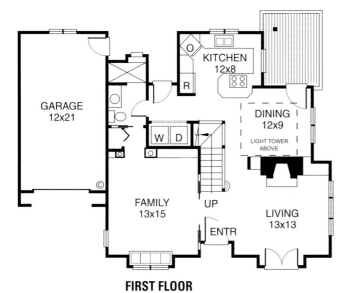

Design 32209

Price Code	B
Total Finished	1,524 sq. ft.
First Finished	877 sq. ft.
Second Finished	647 sq. ft.
Garage Unfinished	281 sq. ft.
Deck Unfinished	141 sq. ft.
Dimensions	44'6"x36'2"
Foundation	Crawlspace
Bedrooms	1
3/4 Baths	2

FIRST FLOOR

GARAGE 12x21

KITCHEN 12x8

DINING 12x9
LIGHT TOWER ABOVE

W D

FAMILY 13x15

UP

LIVING 13x13

ENTR

SECOND FLOOR

MASTER BEDROOM 13x14

SLEEPING PORCH 14x10

DECK

DN

OPEN TO BELOW

OPEN

clean LINES

Constructed with the basic elements of design—one larger rectangle and two smaller rectangles topped by triangular gables—this home is attractive and cost-effective to build. Soaring ceilings, open spaces, and carefully positioned windows work together to make this home seem larger than it already is. The front porch welcomes guests into an air-lock vestibule, which maintains inside heat during cold weather and air conditioning during hot weather. The vestibule opens to the great room, which has a cathedral ceiling and a prominent fireplace. The great room is large enough to accommodate a dining area and opens to the sunroom on one side and kitchen on the other. Stairs lead down from this area to the bedrooms on the walk-out lower floor. Stairs also lead up to the master suite, which includes a private study. This home is designed with a basement foundation. 🏛

above   Where the windows on the porch allow in only low, soft light, the double-hung windows above allow direct sunlight into the two-story great room.

below   Pocket doors lead from the master bedroom to a private study.

right & below The sunny two-story great room is warmed by a fireplace and light from the adjoining sunroom. The staircase leads to the two lower-floor bedrooms, while the adjacent steps lead up to the master suite.

Design 32056

Price Code	D
Total Finished	1,820 sq. ft.
First & Second Finished	1,310 sq. ft.
Lower Finished	510 sq. ft.
Basement Unfinished	840 sq. ft.
Garage Unfinished	672 sq. ft.
Dimensions	81'x52'
Foundation	Basement
Bedrooms	3
Full Baths	2

Please note: The photographed home may have been modified to suit homeowner preferences. If you order plans, you may wish to have a builder or design professional check them against the photographs to confirm construction details.

FIRST & SECOND FLOOR

LOWER FLOOR

woodland RETREAT

above   The character of this picturesque cabin builds on the beauty of its natural surroundings thanks to shingle siding and clean, simple lines.

A t first glance, it's a simple design—a single-floor cabin with a rustic look. But the interior is an open floor plan, created for an easy traffic flow and access to all conveniences. Ideal for a weekend getaway, this home manages to include all the basic conveniences, while maintaining a cozy, country feel. A hall runs along the first floor, leading to a large living room with double doors to the back screen porch. Beside the porch, you'll find a raised deck, the ideal spot for all your outdoor gatherings. Tall windows in the living room create a special spot from which to enjoy the view. L-shape counters give the kitchen ample workspace, while double doors open to a convenient laundry hutch. In the opposite wing, twin bedrooms flank a three-piece bath. This home is designed with basement and crawlspace foundation options. 🏛

below   Natural light streams into the front bedroom. The planked ceiling carries through the pleasing elements of the cabin's refined country interior.

above Vaulted ceilings throughout create a soaring sense of space and openness within this home's modest exterior.

above right Cottage-style cabinetry lends form and function to the kitchen.

right The screen porch offers a comfortable retreat within a retreat.

Design 32122

Price Code	A
Total Finished	1,112 sq. ft.
Main Finished	1,112 sq. ft.
Basement Unfinished	484 sq. ft.
Deck Unfinished	280 sq. ft.
Porch Unfinished	152 sq. ft.
Dimensions	47'x45'6"
Foundation	Basement Crawlspace
Bedrooms	2
Full Baths	1

Please note: The photographed home may have been modified to suit homeowner preferences. If you order plans, you may wish to have a builder or design professional check them against the photographs to confirm construction details.

MAIN FLOOR

PHOTOGRAPHY: BETH SINGER

gabled COTTAGE

above The exterior of this home—a mix of Cape Cod, shingle, and bungalow styling- evokes rustic country traditions.

Triple dormers in the front and rear distinguish the exterior of this home, which wastes no space inside or out. Roomy and light-filled, this ideal starter home provides great shared spaces. The entry leads immediately to the living room, with the staircase tucked into the corner. The living room, dining room, and kitchen share views and one large open space. Traffic flows easily among the spaces, inviting interaction during parties and in everyday activity. A sunroom and laundry room complete the 936-square-foot first floor. A rear veranda and deck provide outdoor living space.

Upstairs, the master suite, which includes a walk-in closet, shares the 916-square-foot second floor with two secondary bedrooms. A full bath divides these two bedrooms. The home is designed with crawlspace and pier/post foundation options. 🏛

below This home's comfortable outdoor spaces include a wide veranda and a deck off the sunroom.

left The large, efficient kitchen takes advantage of space under the stairway, which is supported by a large column. Counters almost completely surround the kitchen and food preparation area including a large bar with room to serve informal meals or to lay out a buffet.

below left A stone fireplace in the living room is flanked by doors that open into an airy, light-filled sunroom, which features a 15-foot ceiling.

Please note: The photographed home may have been modified to suit homeowner preferences. If you order plans, you may wish to have a builder or design professional check them against the photographs to confirm construction details.

SECOND FLOOR

FIRST FLOOR

Design 32291

Price Code	C
Total Finished	1,852 sq. ft.
First Finished	936 sq. ft.
Second Finished	916 sq. ft.
Garage Unfinished	576 sq. ft.
Deck Unfinished	568 sq. ft.
Porch Unfinished	224 sq. ft.
Dimensions	70'x68'
Foundation	Crawlspace Pier/Post
Bedrooms	3
3/4 Baths	3

well-divided SPACE

above Simple country lines with just the right touch of detail enliven this traditional design.

A simple roof line and a basic rectangular footprint make this pretty little three-bedroom home very economical to build. A sheltering front porch extending the length of the facade provides a traditionally welcoming touch. The front door leads into a large living room, which, in turn, is open to the dining room. The dining room offers access to the back yard or a patio and is separated from the kitchen by an island. The open floor plan of the common areas makes the rooms seem larger and more spacious than their already generous proportions. A hall leads from the living room to the bedrooms. The master bedroom offers a real retreat to the homeowner with a private bath and large closet. Two secondary bedrooms at the front of the home share a full hall bath. An optional two-car garage can be built either attached or detached in whichever location best suits your property. This home is designed with basement, slab, and crawlspace foundation options. 🏛

Design 99690

Price Code	A
Total Finished	1,097 sq. ft.
Main Finished	1,097 sq. ft.
Garage Unfinished	461 sq. ft.
Dimensions	56'x35'
Foundation	Basement Crawlspace Slab
Bedrooms	3
Full Baths	1
3/4 Baths	1

OPTIONAL BASEMENT STAIR LOCATION

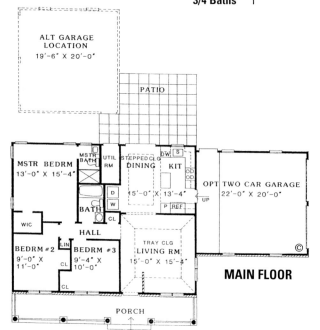

MAIN FLOOR

above Arched windows, keystone details, and a turned-post entry to a covered porch offer plenty of curb appeal in this top-selling plan.

small WONDER

Design 24700

Price Code	A
Total Finished	1,312 sq. ft.
Main Finished	1,312 sq. ft.
Basement Unfinished	1,293 sq. ft.
Garage Unfinished	459 sq. ft.
Deck Unfinished	185 sq. ft.
Porch Unfinished	84 sq. ft.
Dimensions	50'x40'
Foundation	Basement
	Crawlspace
	Slab
Bedrooms	3
Full Baths	2

OPTIONAL CRAWLSPACE/SLAB FOUNDATION

Crawl Access
WH Furn.
Plantng

With its charming details and convenient, practical floor plan, it's no wonder that this lovely, moderate-sized home is our best-selling ranch-style plan. The living room, dining room, and kitchen maintain a sense of separateness due to their careful arrangement within the plan and distinct ceiling treatments, yet remain open to one another to give the public rooms a feeling of spaciousness. The long living room features a fireplace flanked by windows. The dining room has glass doors opening it up to the outdoors. The kitchen includes a built-in pantry opposite the laundry room. The bedrooms are grouped together on the left side of the home. The careful placement of closets, bathrooms, and a short hallway within the bedroom wing offer added privacy by ensuring that none of the bedrooms share a common wall. The master bedroom features a full wall of closet space serving as a buffer between it and the living room. This home is designed with basement, slab, and crawlspace foundation options. 🏛

MAIN FLOOR

Optional Deck

Reveal Clg.
Mstr Br
12-8 x 11-4

Living Rm
13-0 x 19-4

Reveal Clg.
Dining Rm
10-0 x 11-4

Ledge
DW
Kitchen
9-8 x 9-4
Ref

Flat Clg. @ 12'
Beams Above

Railing

Pantry

Laun.

DN

8' Clg.

Linen

Optional Door Location

Foyer

Br 3/Den
10-0 x 11-4

Garage
20-4 x 21-8

Br 2
10-10 x 10-8

Porch

above A two-story bay, long and narrow footprint, and covered porch are hallmarks of turn-of-the-century rowhouse architecture, recreated here with very up-to-date interior spaces.

below The rear deck offers a private retreat without taking up too much space.

rowhouse REVIVAL

This home takes what we love about traditional neighborhood architecture and blends it with open and modern spaces to create a hybrid that works for today's families. The entry leads into the spacious open plan of the first floor, composed of the octagonal formal dining room, kitchen/breakfast area, and family room. In the family room, doors leading to the rear deck flank the fireplace. A peninsula bar extending into the breakfast nook separates the family room from the kitchen. A large pantry in the laundry room adds to the kitchen's efficiency. On the 951-square-foot second floor, the master bedroom claims the entire octagonal space within the upper bay. Its large walk-in closet and five-piece master bath round out the suite. Two secondary bedrooms, one with its own walk-in closet, share a full bath. Ideal for a narrow lot, this home packs in a lot of living space. For outdoor enjoyment, it includes a graceful front porch and a rear deck. This home is designed with a basement foundation. 🏛

left French doors leading to the rear deck flank the fireplace, while floor-to-ceiling windows brighten the adjacent wall of the family room.

below left The homeowner personalized the kitchen with an antique table, which serves as an island, and a raised peninsula counter.

Please note: The photographed home may have been modified to suit homeowner preferences. If you order plans, have a builder or design professional check them against the photographs to confirm construction details.

SECOND FLOOR

left Stained glass surrounds a vanity mirror in the first-floor powder room.

Design 32436

Price Code	A
Total Finished	1,907 sq. ft.
First Finished	956 sq. ft.
Second Finished	951 sq. ft.
Basement Unfinished	965 sq. ft.
Deck Unfinished	112 sq. ft.
Porch Unfinished	126 sq. ft.
Dimensions	28'x48'
Foundation	Basement
Bedrooms	3
Full Baths	2
Half Baths	1

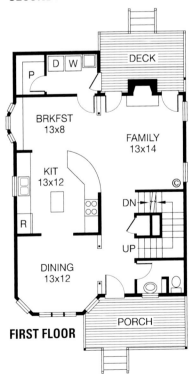

FIRST FLOOR

© William E. Poole Designs

room to GROW

This lovely home offers a classic floor plan updated to include all the amenities the modern family requires. The simple elegance of the Georgian entry leads into an updated center-hall style plan. But in this update, the space usually taken up by the hall has been given over to the great room, reducing construction costs while creating a more livable, up-to-date plan. The front-to-back great room has a fireplace and offers rear access to either a patio or deck. To the right of the foyer, a generous dining room at the front of the house leads back to a well-planned L-shape kitchen with center island and breakfast area. Beyond that, a service wing offers a utility room, two-car garage with storage, and rear stairs leading up to bonus space above the garage. This home is designed with a combination basement/crawlspace foundation. 🏛

above Three-ranked windows balanced with a center paneled door with semi-circular fanlight and elaborate crown and pilasters highlight a mix of Georgian and Adam detailing often found in colonial houses from the late 18th century.

SECOND FLOOR

FIRST FLOOR

Design 57031

Price Code	Call for pricing
Total Finished	1,871 sq. ft.
First Finished	1,028 sq. ft.
Second Finished	843 sq. ft.
Bonus Unfinished	304 sq. ft.
Dimensions	40'x61'
Foundation	Combo Basement/ Crawlspace
Bedrooms	3
Full Baths	2
Half Baths	1

Design 98441

See Order Pages and Index for Info

Units	Single
Price Code	B
Total Finished	1,502 sq. ft.
Main Finished	1,502 sq. ft.
Basement Unfinished	1,555 sq. ft.
Garage Unfinished	448 sq. ft.
Dimensions	51'x50'6"
Foundation	Basement
	Crawlspace
Bedrooms	3
Full Baths	2
Max Ridge Height	24'9"
Roof Framing	Stick
Exterior Walls	2x4

CAD **FILES AVAILABLE**
For more information call
800-235-5700

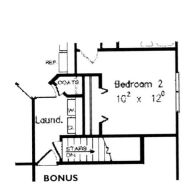

BONUS

Bedroom 2
10² x 12⁰

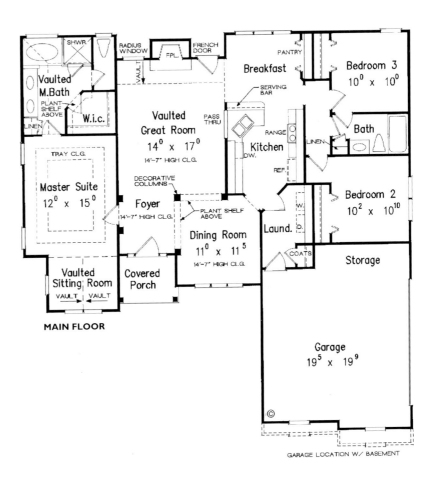

MAIN FLOOR

Design 24721

See Order Pages and Index for Info

Units	Single
Price Code	B
Total Finished	1,539 sq. ft.
Main Finished	1,539 sq. ft.
Basement Unfinished	1,530 sq. ft.
Garage Unfinished	460 sq. ft.
Deck Unfinished	160 sq. ft.
Porch Unfinished	182 sq. ft.
Dimensions	50'x45'4"
Foundation	Basement
	Crawlspace
	Slab
Bedrooms	3
Full Baths	2
Main Ceiling	8'
Max Ridge Height	21'
Roof Framing	Stick
Exterior Walls	2x6

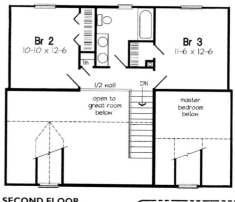

MAIN FLOOR

Design 34602

See Order Pages and Index for Info

Units	Single
Price Code	B
Total Finished	1,560 sq. ft.
First Finished	1,061 sq. ft.
Second Finished	499 sq. ft.
Basement Unfinished	1,061 sq. ft.
Porch Unfinished	339 sq. ft.
Dimensions	44'x34'
Foundation	Basement
	Crawlspace
	Slab
Bedrooms	3
Full Baths	2
Half Baths	1
First Ceiling	8'
Second Ceiling	8'
Max Ridge Height	26'
Roof Framing	Stick
Exterior Walls	2x4, 2x6

CRAWLSPACE/SLAB FOUNDATION OPTION

SECOND FLOOR

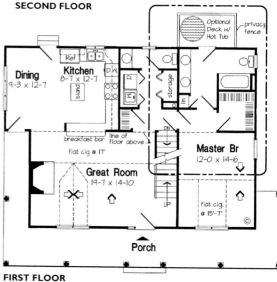

FIRST FLOOR

Order on-line at www.familyhomeplans.com

Design 20220

See Order Pages and Index for Info

MAIN FLOOR

**CRAWLSPACE/SLAB
FOUNDATION OPTION**

Units	Single
Price Code	B
Total Finished	1,568 sq. ft.
Main Finished	1,568 sq. ft.
Basement Unfinished	1,568 sq. ft.
Garage Unfinished	509 sq. ft.
Dimensions	54'x48'4"
Foundation	Basement
	Crawlspace
	Slab
Bedrooms	3
Full Baths	2
Main Ceiling	8'
Vaulted Ceiling	10'
Max Ridge Height	19'
Roof Framing	Stick
Exterior Walls	2x4, 2x6

Design 20198

See Order Pages and Index for Info

PHOTOGRAPHY: COURTESY OF THE DESIGNER

Please note: The photographed home may have been modified to suit homeowner preferences. If you order plans, have a builder or design professional check them against the photograph to confirm actual construction details.

MAIN FLOOR

Units	Single
Price Code	C
Total Finished	1,792 sq. ft.
Main Finished	1,792 sq. ft.
Basement Unfinished	818 sq. ft.
Garage Unfinished	857 sq. ft.
Porch Unfinished	336 sq. ft.
Dimensions	56'x32'
Foundation	Basement
Bedrooms	3
Full Baths	1
3/4 Baths	1
Main Ceiling	8'
Max Ridge Height	25'
Roof Framing	Stick
Exterior Walls	2x4, 2x6

Design **20083**

See Order Pages and Index for Info

PHOTOGRAPHY: COURTESY OF THE DESIGNER

Units	Single
Price Code	B
Total Finished	1,575 sq. ft.
Main Finished	1,575 sq. ft.
Basement Unfinished	1,575 sq. ft.
Garage Unfinished	475 sq. ft.
Dimensions	60'x40'4"
Foundation	Basement
	Crawlspace
	Slab
Bedrooms	3
Full Baths	2
Main Ceiling	8'-10'
Max Ridge Height	19'6"
Roof Framing	Stick
Exterior Walls	2x4, 2x6

REAR ELEVATION

Please note: The photographed home may have been modified to suit homeowner preferences. If you order plans, have a builder or design professional check them against the photograph to confirm actual construction details.

DECK

KIT./BRKFS
11'-8"x13'-10"

LIVING
14'-0"x19'-4"
(10' CLG.)

BEDROOM 3
11'-0"x11'-0"

M.BEDROOM
13'-0"x13'-4"

B.

L.

C.

(VAULT CLG.
7-1/2")

DN

P.

B.

H.

C.

H.

B.

FZ.

DINING RM.
11'-0"x11'-4"

C.

U.

W.

D.

F.

C.

GARAGE
21'-4"x20'-8"

P.

BEDROOM 2
10'-8"x11'-0"

©

DRIVE

MAIN FLOOR

Design 34043

See Order Pages and Index for Info

PHOTOGRAPHY: COURTESY OF THE DESIGNER

Please note: The photographed home may have been modified to suit homeowner preferences. If you order plans, have a builder or design professional check them against the photograph to confirm actual construction details.

Units	Single
Price Code	B
Total Finished	1,583 sq. ft.
Main Finished	1,583 sq. ft.
Basement Unfinished	1,573 sq. ft.
Garage Unfinished	484 sq. ft.
Dimensions	70'x46'
Foundation	Basement
	Crawlspace
	Slab
Bedrooms	3
Full Baths	2
Main Ceiling	8'
Max Ridge Height	20'
Roof Framing	Stick
Exterior Walls	2x4, 2x6

CRAWLSPACE/SLAB FOUNDATION OPTION

MAIN FLOOR

Design 24701

See Order Pages and Index for Info

Units	Single
Price Code	B
Total Finished	1,625 sq. ft.
Main Finished	1,625 sq. ft.
Basement Unfinished	1,625 sq. ft.
Garage Unfinished	455 sq. ft.
Dimensions	54'x48'4"
Foundation	Basement
	Crawlspace
	Slab
Bedrooms	3
Full Baths	2
Main Ceiling	8'-9'
Max Ridge Height	22'
Roof Framing	Stick
Exterior Walls	2x4, 2x6

CRAWLSPACE/SLAB FOUNDATION OPTION

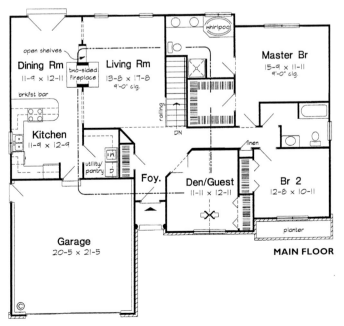

MAIN FLOOR

Design 24717

See Order Pages and Index for Info

Units	Single
Price Code	B
Total Finished	1,642 sq. ft.
Main Finished	1,642 sq. ft.
Basement Unfinished	1,642 sq. ft.
Garage Unfinished	430 sq. ft.
Porch Unfinished	156 sq. ft.
Dimensions	59'x44'
Foundation	Basement
	Crawlspace
	Slab
Bedrooms	3
Full Baths	2
Main Ceiling	9'
Vaulted Ceiling	13'6"
Max Ridge Height	24'
Roof Framing	Stick
Exterior Walls	2x4

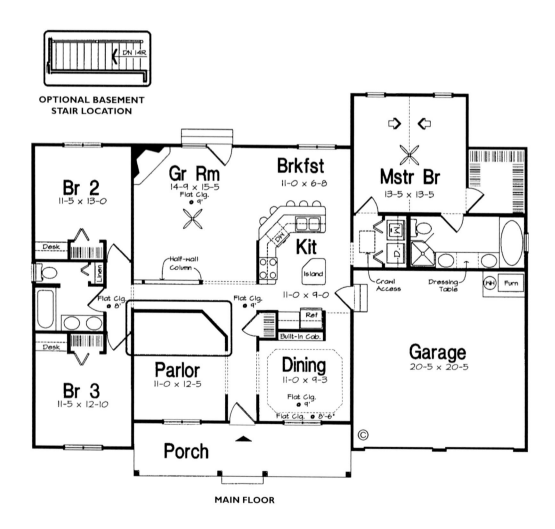

OPTIONAL BASEMENT STAIR LOCATION

DN 14R

Br 2
11-5 x 13-0

Desk

Gr Rm
14-9 x 15-5
Flat Clg. • 9'

Brkfst
11-0 x 6-8

Mstr Br
13-5 x 13-5

Linen

Half-wall Column

Flat Clg. • 8'

Kit
11-0 x 9-0

Island

Crawl Access

Dressing Table

Furn

Flat Clg. • 9'

Ref

Built-In Cab.

Desk

Br 3
11-5 x 12-10

Parlor
11-0 x 12-5

Dining
11-0 x 9-3
Flat Clg. • 9'

Garage
20-5 x 20-5

Flat Clg. • 8-6'

Porch

MAIN FLOOR

Design 94938

See Order Pages and Index for Info

PHOTOGRAPHY: COURTESY OF THE DESIGNER

Units	Single
Price Code	B
Total Finished	1,650 sq. ft.
First Finished	891 sq. ft.
Second Finished	759 sq. ft.
Basement Unfinished	891 sq. ft.
Garage Unfinished	484 sq. ft.
Dimensions	44'x40'
Foundation	Basement
Bedrooms	3
Full Baths	2
Half Baths	1
Max Ridge Height	25'6"
Roof Framing	Stick
Exterior Walls	2x4

* Alternate foundation options available at an additional charge.
Please call 1-800-235-5700 for more information.

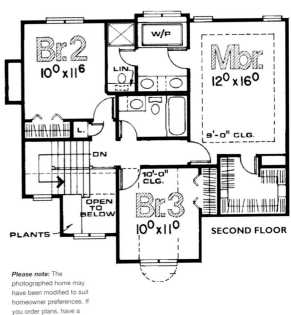

SECOND FLOOR

Please note: The photographed home may have been modified to suit homeowner preferences. If you order plans, have a builder or design professional check them against the photograph to confirm actual construction details.

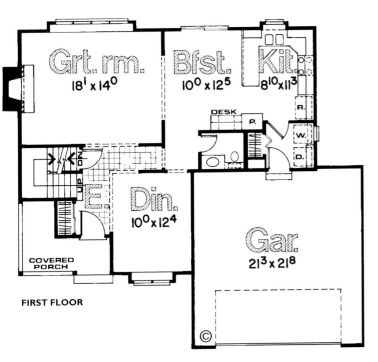

FIRST FLOOR

Design 96506

See Order Pages and Index for Info

Units	Single
Price Code	B
Total Finished	1,654 sq. ft.
Main Finished	1,654 sq. ft.
Garage Unfinished	480 sq. ft.
Porch Unfinished	401 sq. ft.
Dimensions	68'x46'
Foundation	Crawlspace
	Slab
Bedrooms	3
Full Baths	2
Half Baths	1
Main Ceiling	9'
Max Ridge Height	21'
Roof Framing	Stick
Exterior Walls	2x4

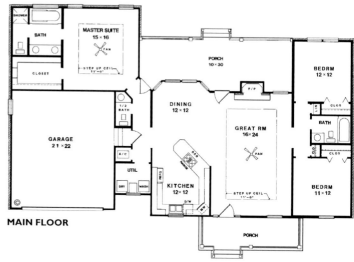

MAIN FLOOR

Design 34029

See Order Pages and Index for Info

ALTERNATE EXTERIOR

PHOTOGRAPHY: JOHN EHRENCLOU & CHARLES BROOKS

Units	Single
Price Code	B
Total Finished	1,686 sq. ft.
Main Finished	1,686 sq. ft.
Basement Unfinished	1,676 sq. ft.
Garage Unfinished	484 sq. ft.
Dimensions	61'x54'
Foundation	Basement
	Crawlspace
	Slab
Bedrooms	3
Full Baths	1
3/4 Baths	1
Main Ceiling	8'
Max Ridge Height	23'
Roof Framing	Stick
Exterior Walls	2x4, 2x6

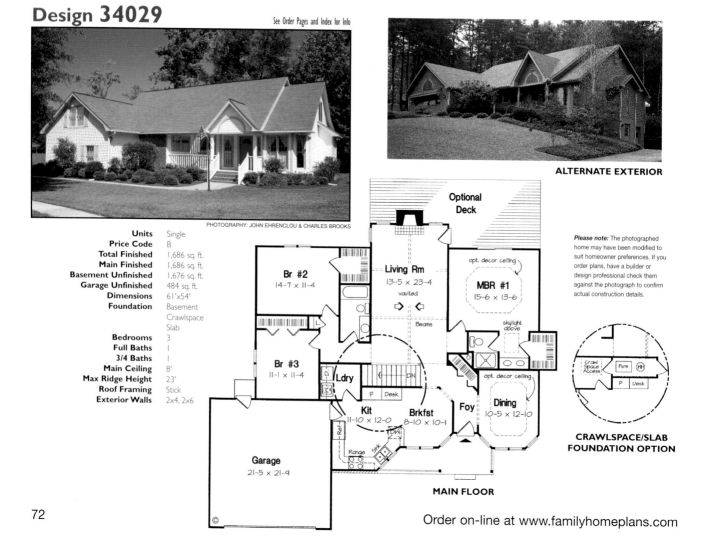

Please note: The photographed home may have been modified to suit homeowner preferences. If you order plans, have a builder or design professional check them against the photograph to confirm actual construction details.

CRAWLSPACE/SLAB FOUNDATION OPTION

MAIN FLOOR

Design 97254

See Order Pages and Index for Info

Units	Single
Price Code	B
Total Finished	1,692 sq. ft.
Main Finished	1,692 sq. ft.
Bonus Unfinished	358 sq. ft.
Basement Unfinished	1,705 sq. ft.
Garage Unfinished	472 sq. ft.
Dimensions	54'x56'6"
Foundation	Basement Crawlspace
Bedrooms	3
Full Baths	2
Max Ridge Height	27'
Roof Framing	Stick
Exterior Walls	2x4

CAD FILES AVAILABLE
For more information call
800-235-7700

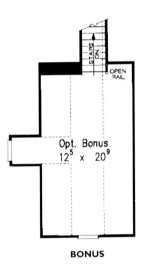

BONUS

Opt. Bonus
12⁵ x 20⁹

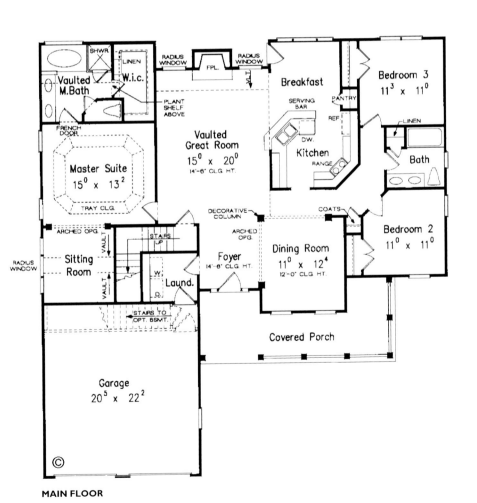

MAIN FLOOR

Design 19422

See Order Pages and Index for Info

PHOTOGRAPHY: MIKE MORELAND

Units	Single
Price Code	B
Total Finished	1,695 sq. ft.
First Finished	1,290 sq. ft.
Second Finished	405 sq. ft.
Garage Unfinished	513 sq. ft.
Porch Unfinished	152 sq. ft.
Dimensions	50'8"×61'8"
Foundation	Basement Crawlspace
Bedrooms	2
Full Baths	2
First Ceiling	9'
Second Ceiling	8'
Max Ridge Height	29'
Roof Framing	Stick/Truss
Exterior Walls	2x4

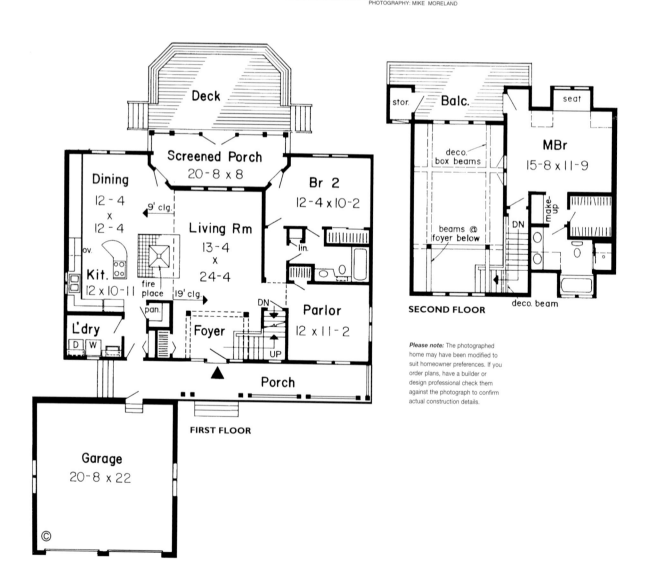

Please note: The photographed home may have been modified to suit homeowner preferences. If you order plans, have a builder or design professional check them against the photograph to confirm actual construction details.

Design 98456

See Order Pages and Index for Info

Units	Single
Price Code	B
Total Finished	1,715 sq. ft.
Main Finished	1,715 sq. ft.
Basement Unfinished	1,715 sq. ft.
Garage Unfinished	450 sq. ft.
Dimensions	55'x51'6"
Foundation	Basement
	Crawlspace
	Slab
Bedrooms	3
Full Baths	2
Main Ceiling	9'1"
Max Ridge Height	25'
Roof Framing	Stick
Exterior Walls	2x4

CAD FILES AVAILABLE
For more information call
800-235-5700

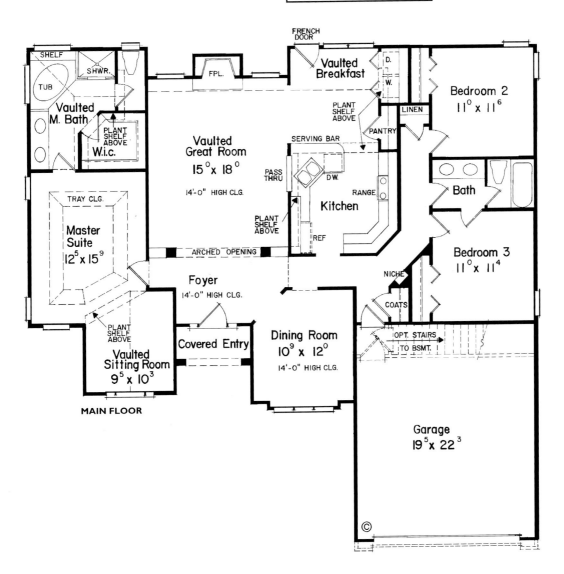

Design 20100

See Order Pages and Index for Info

PHOTOGRAPHY: JOHN EHRENCLOU

Units	Single
Price Code	B
Total Finished	1,737 sq. ft.
Main Finished	1,737 sq. ft.
Basement Unfinished	1,727 sq. ft.
Garage Unfinished	484 sq. ft.
Dimensions	72'4"x43'
Foundation	Basement Crawlspace Slab
Bedrooms	3
Full Baths	2
Main Ceiling	8'
Max Ridge Height	21'
Roof Framing	Stick
Exterior Walls	2x6

REAR ELEVATION

Please note: The photographed home may have been modified to suit homeowner preferences. If you order plans, have a builder or design professional check them against the photograph to confirm actual construction details.

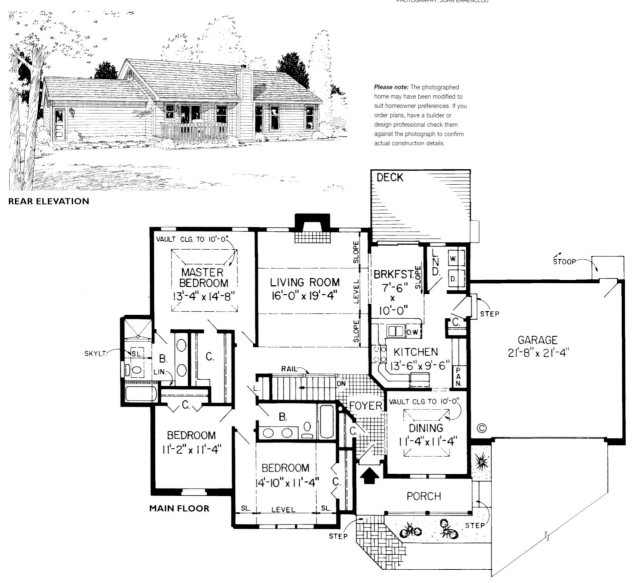

1,501-2,000 SQ. FT.

Design 10839

See Order Pages and Index for Info

PHOTOGRAPHY: COURTESY OF THE DESIGNER

REAR ELEVATION

Units	Single
Price Code	B
Total Finished	1,750 sq. ft.
Main Finished	1,750 sq. ft.
Basement Unfinished	1,083 sq. ft.
Garage Unfinished	796 sq. ft.
Porch Unfinished	100 sq. ft.
Dimensions	66'x52'
Foundation	Basement
	Crawlspace
	Slab
Bedrooms	2
Full Baths	2
Main Ceiling	8'
Max Ridge Height	24'6"
Roof Framing	Stick
Exterior Walls	2x4, 2x6

Please note: The photographed home may have been modified to suit homeowner preferences. If you order plans, have a builder or design professional check them against the photograph to confirm actual construction details.

CRAWLSPACE/SLAB FOUNDATION OPTION

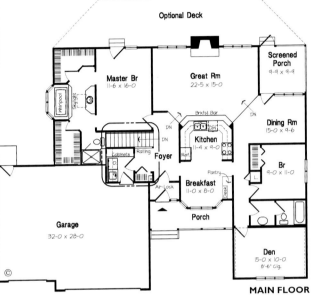

MAIN FLOOR

Design 97757

See Order Pages and Index for Info

Units	Single
Price Code	B
Total Finished	1,755 sq. ft.
Main Finished	1,755 sq. ft.
Basement Unfinished	1,725 sq. ft.
Garage Unfinished	796 sq. ft.
Deck Unfinished	44 sq. ft.
Porch Unfinished	138 sq. ft.
Dimensions	78'6"x47'7"
Foundation	Basement
Bedrooms	3
Full Baths	2
Main Ceiling	8'
Max Ridge Height	22'
Roof Framing	Truss
Exterior Walls	2x4

MAIN FLOOR

See thousands more plans at www.familyhomeplans.com

Design 34901

See Order Pages and Index for Info

PHOTOGRAPHY: LAURIE SALOMON

Units	Single
Price Code	C
Total Finished	1,763 sq. ft.
First Finished	909 sq. ft.
Second Finished	854 sq. ft.
Basement Unfinished	899 sq. ft.
Garage Unfinished	491 sq. ft.
Dimensions	48'x44'
Foundation	Basement
	Crawlspace
	Slab
Bedrooms	3
Full Baths	1
3/4 Baths	1
Half Baths	1
First Ceiling	8'
Second Ceiling	8'
Tray Ceiling	9'
Max Ridge Height	29'
Roof Framing	Stick
Exterior Walls	2x4, 2x6

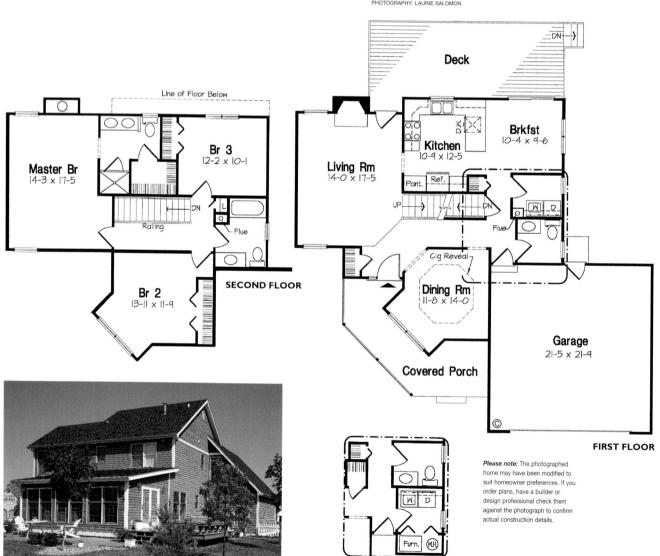

SECOND FLOOR

Master Br
14-3 x 17-5

Br 3
12-2 x 10-1

Br 2
13-11 x 11-9

Line of Floor Below

Railing

DN

Flue

Deck

Kitchen
10-9 x 12-5

Brkfst
10-4 x 9-6

Living Rm
14-0 x 17-5

Pant.

Ref.

UP

DN

Flue

W D

Clg Reveal

Dining Rm
11-8 x 14-0

Garage
21-5 x 21-9

Covered Porch

FIRST FLOOR

CRAWLSPACE/SLAB
FOUNDATION OPTION

Furn.   MUH

Please note: The photographed home may have been modified to suit homeowner preferences. If you order plans, have a builder or design professional check them against the photograph to confirm actual construction details.

REAR ELEVATION

Design 24714

See Order Pages and Index for Info

Units	Single
Price Code	C
Total Finished	1,771 sq. ft.
Main Finished	1,771 sq. ft.
Basement Unfinished	1,194 sq. ft.
Garage Unfinished	517 sq. ft.
Porch Unfinished	106 sq. ft.
Dimensions	54'×50'
Foundation	Slab
	Crawlspace
	Combo Basement/
	Crawlspace
Bedrooms	2
Full Baths	2
Main Ceiling	8'
Vaulted Ceiling	13'6"
Max Ridge Height	23'6"
Roof Framing	Stick
Exterior Walls	2x4

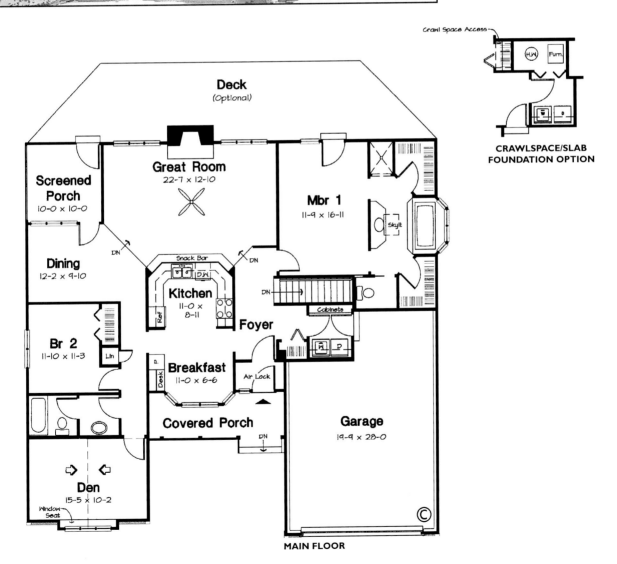

CRAWLSPACE/SLAB
FOUNDATION OPTION

MAIN FLOOR

1,501-2,000 Sq. Ft.

Design 98464

See Order Pages and Index for Info

Units	Single
Price Code	C
Total Finished	1,779 sq. ft.
Main Finished	1,779 sq. ft.
Basement Unfinished	1,818 sq. ft.
Garage Unfinished	499 sq. ft.
Dimensions	57'x56'4"
Foundation	Basement
	Crawlspace
Bedrooms	3
Full Baths	2
Main Ceiling	9'
Max Ridge Height	24'6"
Roof Framing	Stick
Exterior Walls	2x4

MAIN FLOOR

OPTIONAL BASEMENT STAIR LOCATION

Design 24610

See Order Pages and Index for Info

Units	Single
Price Code	C
Total Finished	1,785 sq. ft.
First Finished	891 sq. ft.
Second Finished	894 sq. ft.
Basement Unfinished	891 sq. ft.
Garage Unfinished	534 sq. ft.
Dimensions	46'8"x35'8"
Foundation	Basement
	Crawlspace
	Slab
Bedrooms	3
Full Baths	1
3/4 Baths	1
Half Baths	1
First Ceiling	8'
Second Ceiling	8'
Max Ridge Height	28'
Roof Framing	Stick
Exterior Walls	2x4

REAR ELEVATION

SECOND FLOOR

FIRST FLOOR

Design 65380

See Order Pages and Index for Info

Units	Single
Price Code	C
Total Finished	1,832 sq. ft.
First Finished	1,212 sq. ft.
Second Finished	620 sq. ft.
Basement Unfinished	1,212 sq. ft.
Dimensions	38'x40'
Foundation	Basement
Bedrooms	3
Full Baths	2
First Ceiling	8'
Max Ridge Height	26'4"

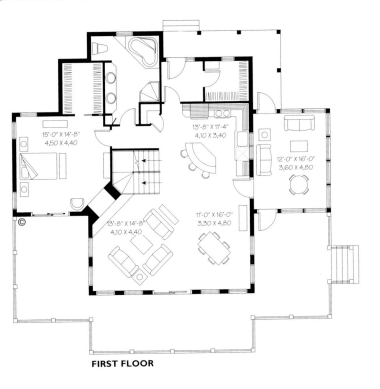

FIRST FLOOR

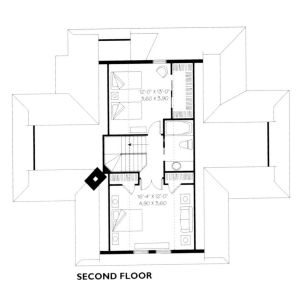

SECOND FLOOR

Design 92220

See Order Pages and Index for Info

Units	Single
Price Code	C
Total Finished	1,830 sq. ft.
Main Finished	1,830 sq. ft.
Garage Unfinished	759 sq. ft.
Deck Unfinished	315 sq. ft.
Porch Unfinished	390 sq. ft.
Dimensions	75'×52'3"
Foundation	Basement
	Crawlspace
	Slab
Bedrooms	3
Full Baths	2
Max Ridge Height	27'3"
Roof Framing	Stick
Exterior Walls	2x4

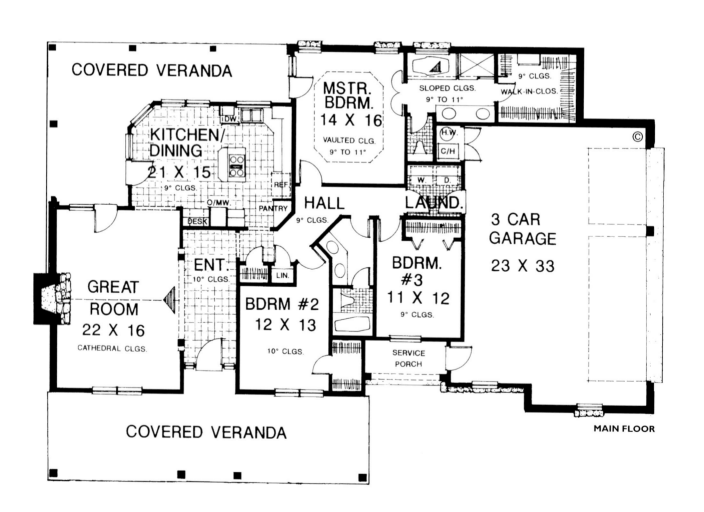

COVERED VERANDA

KITCHEN/DINING
21 X 15
9° CLGS.

MSTR. BDRM.
14 X 16
VAULTED CLG.
9° TO 11°

SLOPED CLGS.
9° TO 11°

9° CLGS.
WALK-IN-CLOS.

H.W.
C/H

W. D.

HALL
9° CLGS.

LAUND.

3 CAR GARAGE
23 X 33

DESK
PANTRY
REF.

ENT.
10° CLGS.

LIN.

BDRM. #3
11 X 12
9° CLGS.

GREAT ROOM
22 X 16
CATHEDRAL CLGS.

BDRM #2
12 X 13
10° CLGS.

SERVICE PORCH

COVERED VERANDA

MAIN FLOOR

Design 34031

See Order Pages and Index for Info

Units	Single
Price Code	C
Total Finished	1,831 sq. ft.
Main Finished	1,831 sq. ft.
Basement Unfinished	1,831 sq. ft.
Garage Unfinished	484 sq. ft.
Dimensions	60'x52'
Foundation	Basement
	Crawlspace
	Slab
Bedrooms	3
Full Baths	2
Half Baths	1
Main Ceiling	8'
Max Ridge Height	22'
Roof Framing	Stick
Exterior Walls	2x4, 2x6

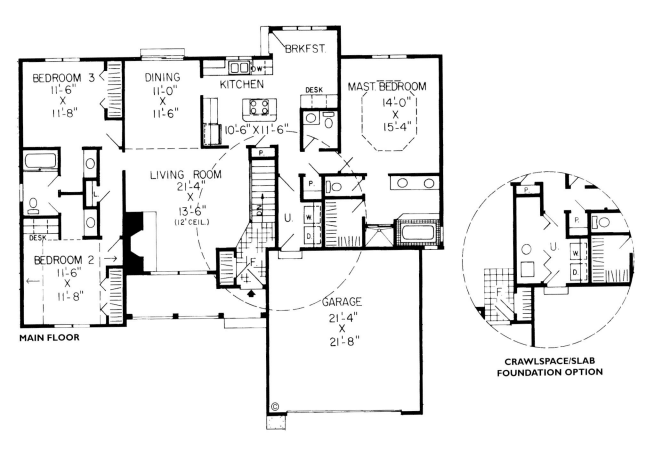

MAIN FLOOR

**CRAWLSPACE/SLAB
FOUNDATION OPTION**

Design 98425

See Order Pages and Index for Info

Units	Single
Price Code	C
Total Finished	1,845 sq. ft.
Main Finished	1,845 sq. ft.
Bonus Unfinished	409 sq. ft.
Basement Unfinished	1,845 sq. ft.
Garage Unfinished	529 sq. ft.
Dimensions	56'x60'
Foundation	Basement
	Crawlspace
Bedrooms	3
Full Baths	2
Half Baths	1
Main Ceiling	9'
Max Ridge Height	26'6"
Roof Framing	Stick
Exterior Walls	2x4

CAD FILES AVAILABLE
For more information call
800-235-5700

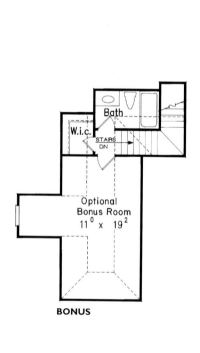

BONUS

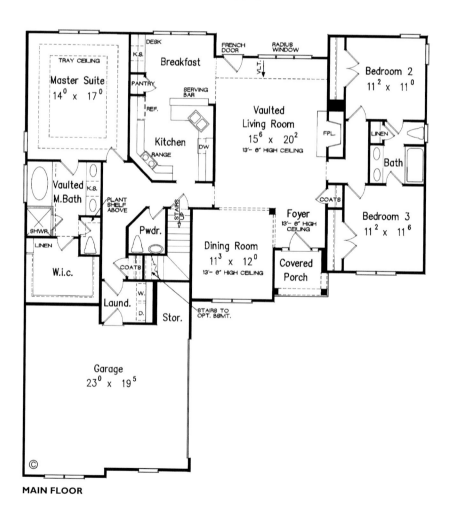

MAIN FLOOR

Design 57093

See Order Pages and Index for Info

Units	Single
Price Code	Please call for pricing
Total Finished	1,866 sq. ft.
First Finished	1,314 sq. ft.
Second Finished	552 sq. ft.
Bonus Unfinished	398 sq. ft.
Dimensions	44'2"x62'
Foundation	Crawlspace
Bedrooms	3
Full Baths	2
Half Baths	1
Max Ridge Height	27'
Roof Framing	Stick
Exterior Walls	2x4

Hot New Design

STORAGE

BEDROOM 2
13'-6" X 11'-7"

BEDROOM 3
13'-4" X 13'-0"

LINEN

DOWN

BATH 2

OPEN TO BELOW

ROOF AREA

STORAGE

FUTURE REC. ROOM
14'-8" X 23'-0"

SECOND FLOOR

REAR ELEVATION

DECK / TERRACE AREA

MASTER BEDROOM
13'-4" X 15'-0"

GREAT ROOM
21'-4" X 15'-0"

WARDROBE
7'-0" X 7'-0"

MASTER BATH

DINING ROOM
13'-10" X 10'-6"

WHIRLPOOL TUB

LINE OF WALL ABOVE

FOYER

BAR

PANTRY

POWDER ROOM

KITCHEN
12'-6" X 12'-6"

UTILITY
9'-2" X 9'-0"

PORCH
8'-0" X 6'-0"

© William E. Poole Designs, Inc.

2 CAR GARAGE
22'-0" X 23'-0"

STOOP

FIRST FLOOR

Design 10785

See Order Pages and Index for Info

PHOTOGRAPHY: COURTESY OF THE DESIGNER

Units	Single
Price Code	C
Total Finished	1,907 sq. ft.
First Finished	1,269 sq. ft.
Second Finished	638 sq. ft.
Basement Unfinished	1,269 sq. ft.
Dimensions	47'x39'
Foundation	Basement
	Crawlspace
	Slab
Bedrooms	3
Full Baths	2
Half Baths	1
First Ceiling	8'
Second Ceiling	8'
Max Ridge Height	24'
Roof Framing	Stick
Exterior Walls	2x6

**CRAWLSPACE/SLAB
FOUNDATION OPTION**

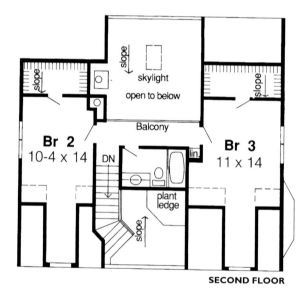

SECOND FLOOR

Please note: The photographed home may have been modified to suit homeowner preferences. If you order plans, have a builder or design professional check them against the photograph to confirm actual construction details.

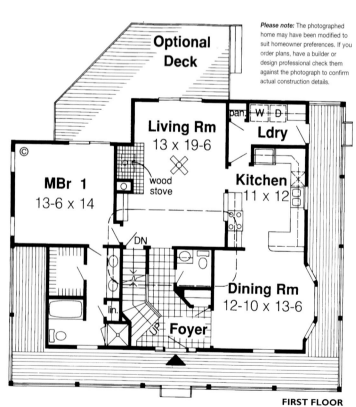

FIRST FLOOR

REAR ELEVATION

Design 20501

See Order Pages and Index for Info

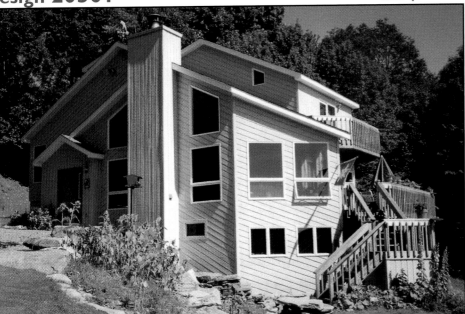

PHOTOGRAPHY: COURTESY OF THE DESIGNER

Units	Single
Price Code	C
Total Finished	1,908 sq. ft.
First Finished	1,316 sq. ft.
Second Finished	592 sq. ft.
Dimensions	39'x48'
Foundation	Basement
	Crawlspace
Bedrooms	3
Full Baths	2
Max Ridge Height	34'
Roof Framing	Stick
Exterior Walls	2x6

SIDE ELEVATION

attic access   knee space

shelf

linen   step   shelf

Please note: The photographed home may have been modified to suit homeowner preferences. If you order plans, have a builder or design professional check them against the photograph to confirm actual construction details.

DN   UP   36" wall
books

Mstr. Suite
17-8 x 16-4   slope   8'-0"
ceiling
slope

Balcony

SECOND FLOOR

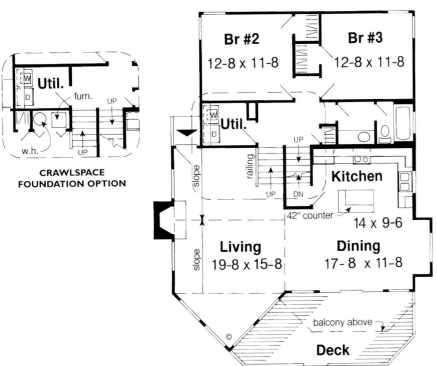

Br #2
12-8 x 11-8

Br #3
12-8 x 11-8

W

Util.

UP

UP   DN

Kitchen

42" counter   14 x 9-6

Living
19-8 x 15-8

Dining
17-8 x 11-8

railing   slope   slope

balcony above

Deck

FIRST FLOOR

W
D
Util.   furn.   UP

w.h.   UP

CRAWLSPACE FOUNDATION OPTION

Design 98435

See Order Pages and Index for Info

Units	Single
Price Code	C
Total Finished	1,945 sq. ft.
Main Finished	1,945 sq. ft.
Dimensions	56'6"x52'6"
Foundation	Basement
	Crawlspace
Bedrooms	4
Full Baths	2
Main Ceiling	9'
Max Ridge Height	26'4"
Roof Framing	Stick
Exterior Walls	2x4

CAD **FILES AVAILABLE**
For more information call
800-235-7000

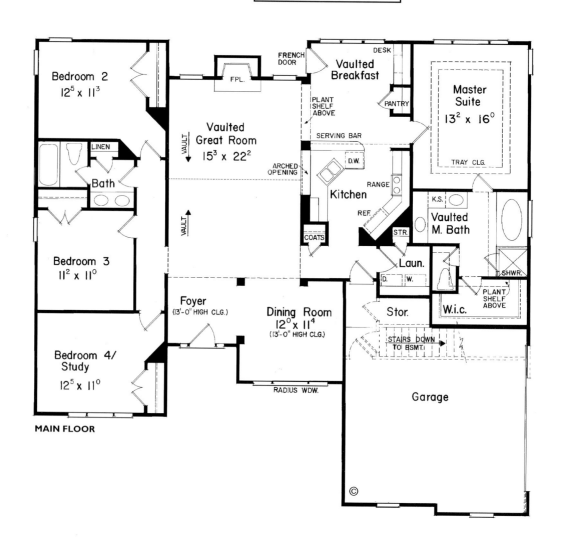

MAIN FLOOR

Design 99115

See Order Pages and Index for Info

Units	Single
Price Code	C
Total Finished	1,947 sq. ft.
Main Finished	1,947 sq. ft.
Basement Unfinished	1,947 sq. ft.
Dimensions	69'8"x46'
Foundation	Basement
Bedrooms	3
Full Baths	2
Half Baths	1
Main Ceiling	8'
Max Ridge Height	22'4"
Roof Framing	Truss
Exterior Walls	2x6

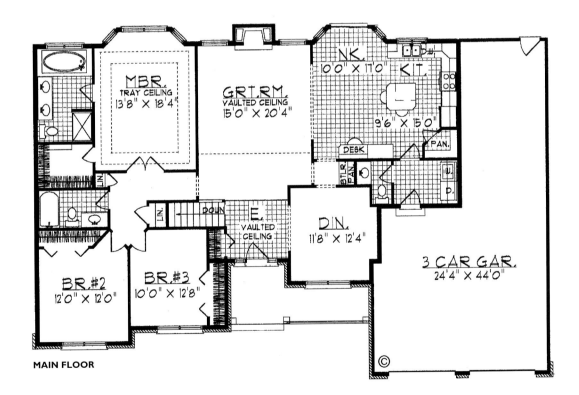

MAIN FLOOR

Design **57057**

See Order Pages and Index for Info

Units	Single
Price Code	Please call for pricing
Total Finished	1,973 sq. ft.
Main Finished	1,973 sq. ft.
Bonus Unfinished	368 sq. ft.
Dimensions	64'10"x58'2"
Foundation	Basement Crawlspace
Bedrooms	3
Full Baths	2
First Ceiling	9'
Max Ridge Height	26'
Roof Framing	Stick
Exterior Walls	2x6

Hot New Design

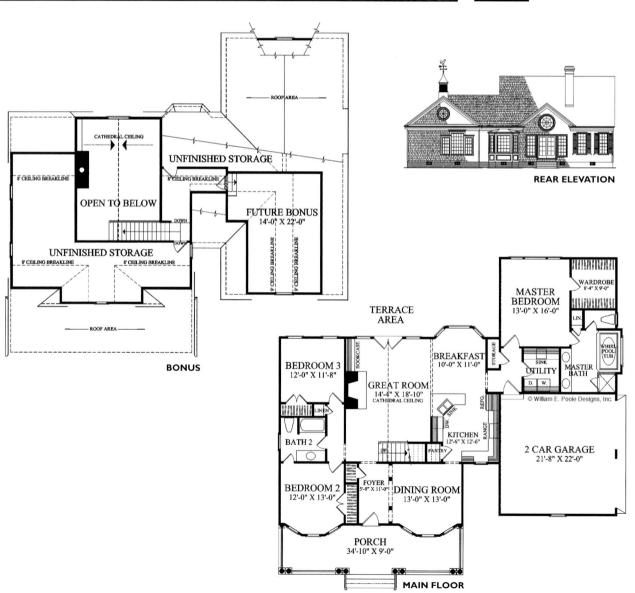

Design 24400

See Order Pages and Index for Info

PHOTOGRAPHY: COURTESY OF THE DESIGNER

Units	Single
Price Code	C
Total Finished	1,978 sq. ft.
First Finished	1,034 sq. ft.
Second Finished	944 sq. ft.
Basement Unfinished	984 sq. ft.
Garage Unfinished	675 sq. ft.
Dimensions	67'6"x39'6"
Foundation	Basement
	Crawlspace
	Slab
Bedrooms	4
Full Baths	2
Half Baths	1
First Ceiling	9'
Second Ceiling	8'
Max Ridge Height	29'
Roof Framing	Stick
Exterior Walls	2x4, 2x6

REAR ELEVATION

crawl access

Dining

Furn. w/h

**CRAWLSPACE/SLAB
FOUNDATION OPTION**

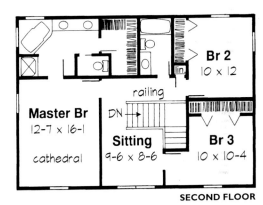

Br 2
10 x 12

railing

Master Br
12-7 x 16-1

DN

cathedral

Sitting
9-6 x 8-6

Br 3
10 x 10-4

SECOND FLOOR

MASTER BATH OPTION

Please note: The photographed home may have been modified to suit homeowner preferences. If you order plans, have a builder or design professional check them against the photograph to confirm actual construction details.

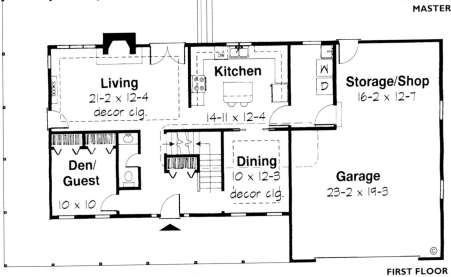

Living
21-2 x 12-4
decor clg.

Kitchen
14-11 x 12-4

Storage/Shop
16-2 x 12-7

**Den/
Guest**
10 x 10

Dining
10 x 12-3
decor clg.

Garage
23-2 x 19-3

FIRST FLOOR

Design 19299

See Order Pages and Index for Info

PHOTOGRAPHY: STEVE GRAHAM

Units	Single
Price Code	C
Total Finished	1,980 sq. ft.
Main Finished	1,980 sq. ft.
Garage Unfinished	484 sq. ft.
Dimensions	64'8"x55'
Foundation	Combo Basement/ Crawlspace
Bedrooms	3
Full Baths	2
Half Baths	1
Main Ceiling	8'
Max Ridge Height	21'
Roof Framing	Stick
Exterior Walls	2x4

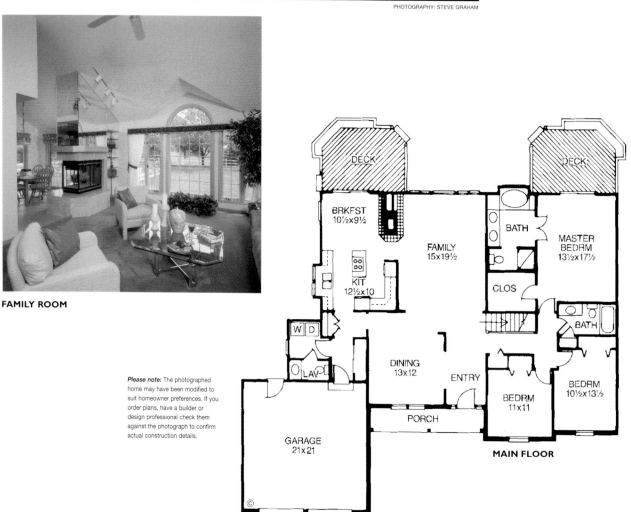

FAMILY ROOM

Please note: The photographed home may have been modified to suit homeowner preferences. If you order plans, have a builder or design professional check them against the photograph to confirm actual construction details.

Design **65234**

See Order Pages and Index for Info

See Order Pages and Index for Info

Units	Single
Price Code	E
Total Finished	1,995 sq. ft.
First Finished	1,525 sq. ft.
Second Finished	470 sq. ft.
Basement Unfinished	1,525 sq. ft.
Garage Unfinished	596 sq. ft.
Dimensions	56'x53'2"
Foundation	Basement
Bedrooms	3
Full Baths	2
Half Baths	1
First Ceiling	9'
Second Ceiling	8'
Max Ridge Height	29'9"
Roof Framing	Truss
Exterior Walls	2x6

FIRST FLOOR

SECOND FLOOR

Design **65368**

See Order Pages and Index for Info

REAR ELEVATION

Units	Single
Price Code	C
Total Finished	1,995 sq. ft.
First Finished	1,525 sq. ft.
Second Finished	470 sq. ft.
Basement Unfinished	1,525 sq. ft.
Garage Unfinished	623 sq. ft.
Deck Unfinished	81 sq. ft.
Porch Unfinished	113 sq. ft.
Dimensions	56'x53'
Foundation	Basement
Bedrooms	2
Full Baths	2
Half Baths	1
First Ceiling	8'
Second Ceiling	8'
Max Ridge Height	29'9"
Roof Framing	Truss
Exterior Walls	2x6

SECOND FLOOR

FIRST FLOOR

Design **94904**

See Order Pages and Index for Info

PHOTOGRAPHY: COURTESY OF THE DESIGNER

Units	Single
Price Code	C
Total Finished	1,998 sq. ft.
First Finished	1,093 sq. ft.
Second Finished	905 sq. ft.
Basement Unfinished	1,093 sq. ft.
Garage Unfinished	527 sq. ft.
Dimensions	55'4"x37'8"
Foundation	Basement
Bedrooms	3
Full Baths	2
Half Baths	1
First Ceiling	8'
Second Ceiling	8'
Max Ridge Height	29'
Roof Framing	Stick
Exterior Walls	2x4

* Alternate foundation options available at an additional charge.
Please call 1-800-235-5700 for more information.

Please note: The photographed home may have been modified to suit homeowner preferences. If you order plans, have a builder or design professional check them against the photograph to confirm actual construction details.

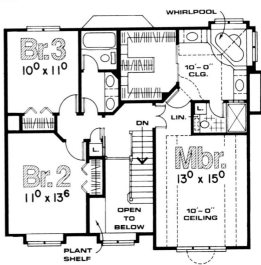

SECOND FLOOR

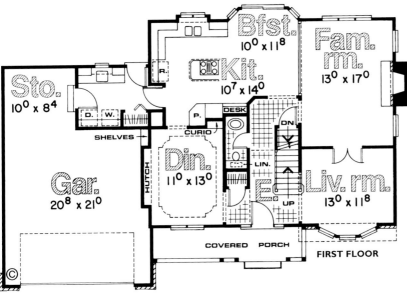

FIRST FLOOR

kitchen LIGHTING

above Recessed downlights provide even illumination over the work spaces in this bright kitchen. (Photo courtesy of The Sater Design Collection.)

Kitchens today are more than places to prepare meals. The room now ranks as the heart of the home and center of family activity.

"The kitchen has become the hub of the house," says Barry Levett, owner and president of House of Lights in Mayfield Heights, Ohio. "Families today truly live in the kitchen. Kids study there; parents pay the bills and write checks there; everyone reads the morning paper in the kitchen; families eat their meals there."

Such multi-tasking kitchens demand equally versatile lighting. A single 100-watt fixture centered in the kitchen's ceiling is no longer sufficient.

"I see people every day who are saddled with one light in the middle of the kitchen," says Geoff Dent, president of Dent Electrical Supply in Danbury, Connecticut. "Most of the work in a kitchen is done around the perimeter of the room. This means that, with only one central fixture, you're working in your own shadow. To make matters worse, the fixture is usually undersized, and we all need more light as we get older."

The Right Light for the Job

The best lighting for your kitchen depends on the size and complexity of the room. Small kitchens may require only a central ceiling fixture and task lighting tucked under a cabinet. More elaborate kitchens will demand a blend of general, task, and accent lighting, according to the American Lighting Association.

"Lights have specific functions, whether it's to accent a specific area, create general ambience, focus on a task, or wash a wall," says Monty Gilbertson, CLC, manager and buyer for Lighting Design by Wettsteins in Lacrosse, Wisconsin. "You are seeing all types incorporated into the kitchen."

Determine what you want the lights to do. Functional fixtures provide well-diffused general lighting that's perfect for moving about the room safely, peering inside drawers and cabinets, and performing chores. While large, surface fluorescents have been

above The latest looks revolve around low-voltage, industrial style. (Photo courtesy of The American Lighting Association)

popular in the past, the latest looks revolve around recessed lights and low voltage, industrial styles, often with a metal finish.

Recessed downlights assure even illumination. Installed over the stove and sink areas, they create adequate task lighting for cooking and cleaning. "When you add new lights over the sink or stove, the whole area comes alive," says Levett.

The kitchen table is another family focal point. A decorative pendant, operating with a dimmer control, will provide sufficient lighting. "People want to make a statement by hanging a pendant, then backing it up with task lighting at the counter," says Gilbertson.

Pendant lighting installed over islands or peninsulas gets the job done. "Light over the island is not only functional, but beautiful," says Dent. "Even people who use recessed lights throughout the kitchen can introduce some color and style over the island. I personally prefer several smaller pendants."

Consider a decorative fixture with three lights. "A trio over an island provides good light," says Levett. "It breaks up the kitchen but you can still see through it."

Make Sure You Have Enough Circuits

No matter how many lights you install in your kitchen, the American Lighting Association recommends circuiting them separately so the lighting is zoned. This allows you to create ambience by mixing the various lights you turn on.

"Lights above the cabinets should be soft and low-voltage," suggests Gilbertson. "The light over the sink should have its own switch. Same with the lights over the island and those over counters. You will be pleased with the results."

below Decorative pendants illuminate the center island while task lighting over the counters and range ensure that no one gets left in the dark. (Photo courtesy of The American Lighting Association)

For more information about great ideas for kitchen lighting, visit www.americanlightingassoc.com, the website of the American Lighting Association, a not-for-profit association of leading manufacturers, retail lighting showrooms, and sales representatives in the U.S. and Canada.

PHOTOGRAPHY: RICK TAYLOR

casual ELEGANCE

With its wide-open spaces and easy traffic flow, this plan is ideal for entertaining. The front door with sidelights and an arched transom ushers guests inside where they have an immediate view of the formal dining room to the left and straight ahead to the family room. The family room's fireplace and built-ins are set to the side to allow a bank of windows to take over the rear wall.

In the kitchen, the cooktop island helps block the view of the food preparation area from the breakfast area. Past the breakfast area, French doors open onto a screen porch, extending the dining space in nice weather. Just off the screen porch, a corner deck offers additional outdoor living space. Other rooms on the 2,442-square-foot first floor include the master suite and a study.

Two bedrooms and two full baths are located on the 871-square-foot second floor. The bonus room adds 480 square feet. The lower level (not shown) adds an additional 2,442 square feet. This home is designed with a basement foundation. 🏛

above Mixed siding materials, clapboards and stone, create a rich texture. The long, shady porch is a welcoming spot to greet guests and neighbors.

below The entry and the upstairs hall remain light and open thanks to the entry's two-story height capped by a dormer. The doorway at left opens to the study.

family-style SPACES

left A long kitchen island includes a cooktop and prep sink and helps distinguish the kitchen area from the adjacent open breakfast area. The windows over the sink look out over the rear deck.

below The bay window in the master bedroom opens up the space for a cozy sitting area.

Please note: The photographed home may have been modified to suit homeowner preferences. If you order plans, you may wish to have a builder or design professional check them against the photographs to confirm construction details.

Design 32358

Price Code	I
Total Finished	5,755 sq. ft.
First Finished	2,442 sq. ft.
Second Finished	871 sq. ft.
Lower Finished	2,442 sq. ft.
Bonus Unfinished	480 sq. ft.
Garage Unfinished	935 sq. ft.
Deck Unfinished	307 sq. ft.
Porch Unfinished	442 sq. ft.
Dimensions	72'6x76'10"
Foundation	Basement
Bedrooms	3
Full Baths	3
Half Baths	1

FIRST FLOOR

SECOND FLOOR

scenic HOME

On the main level at the heart of the home is the kitchen, which receives morning sun through windows tucked into a small dormer over the home's front entry. The layout of the home radiates around the kitchen, which contains professional-style appliances and a walk-in pantry for extra storage space. Behind the kitchen is a small breakfast nook for casual meals. The home is designed for single-level living, with a master suite and laundry on the main level. At one end of the home, the master suite includes a luxurious bath with a relaxing corner tub. At the other end of the main level lies the great room, which is separated from the kitchen by a raised counter. A large bank of transom-topped windows floods the room with light, while a vaulted ceiling lends a sense of space. The great room features a fireplace that is flanked on one side by built-in cabinets that can be used for wood storage or an entertainment center.

The lower level is designed for fun and guests, and includes three bedrooms, a full bath, and a large recreation area with bar and fireplace. A doorway at the foot of the stairs can close off the lower level to keep noise to a minimum. This home is designed with a basement foundation. 🏛

above Natural colors in the stone, redwood siding, and shingles help the home blend with its environment. The low, sweeping roofline allows it to maintain an unobtrusive profile. The home's design offers all types of views whether from the master suite's bump-out area, the breakfast nook, or the deck.

below Large windows flood the great room with sunlight to highlight the birch and cherry woodwork. A vaulted ceiling adds volume and detail without overpowering the room.

above   Set into a sunny rear alcove just behind the kitchen, the breakfast nook has a wide-open feel thanks to transom-topped windows and open-railing stairs.

left   Cherry wood cabinets and hardwood flooring glow in the abundant natural light that floods the kitchen. Contemporary fixtures and a decorative ceiling add modernity to elegance.

Design 32375

Price Code	L
Total Finished	4,022 sq. ft.
Main Finished	2,019 sq. ft.
Lower Finished	2,003 sq. ft.
Garage Unfinished	783 sq. ft.
Deck Unfinished	204 sq. ft.
Porch Unfinished	388 sq. ft.
Dimensions	73'8"x55'8"
Foundation	Basement
Bedrooms	4
Full Baths	2
Half Baths	1

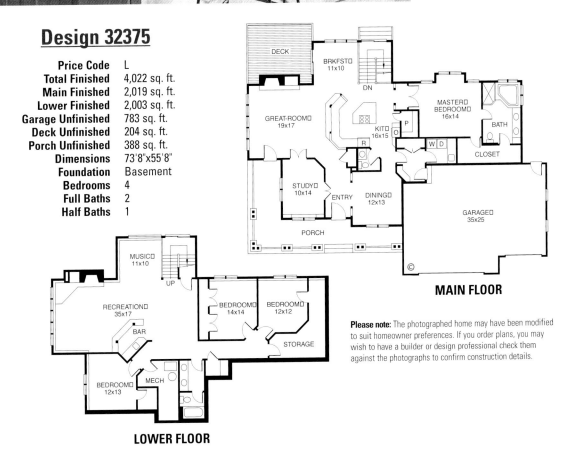

MAIN FLOOR

LOWER FLOOR

Please note: The photographed home may have been modified to suit homeowner preferences. If you order plans, you may wish to have a builder or design professional check them against the photographs to confirm construction details.

PHOTOGRAPHY: COURTESY OF THE DESIGNER

arts & crafts COMFORT

This is not a typical Arts and Crafts update in which only a nod is given to the style; this home speaks of the Craftsman tradition throughout. Just inside the foyer is a beautifully made built-in bench flanked by see-through display cabinets with leaded-glass doors. While the dining room is rich in traditional Craftsman touches, such as the built-in china cabinets, box-beams, stenciling, and rich natural wood tones, straight across the hall, the great room is an altogether different story. The great room features the same sense of tradition, yet is somehow a bit more contemporary. On the 2,171-square-foot second floor, the master suite, with impressive bath and room-size walk-in closets, fills almost the entire front of the plan. A guest suite completes the area. To the rear, two secondary bedrooms share a full bath, each with access to their own vanity. Four porches and a sunroom add outdoor living space and a three-car garage includes additional storage space. This home is designed with a crawlspace foundation. 🏛

above Low eaves, earthy colors, natural siding, and exposed rafter tails are trademark elements of Arts and Crafts design.

below At the front of the home, the private study brings out the best of Craftsman design.

above Box beams, built-in china cabinets with leaded-glass doors, stenciling, and lots of natural wood provide the dining room with tradition and ambiance.

left The Craftsman tradition of natural wood finishes reaches a contemporary zenith in this large gourmet kitchen.

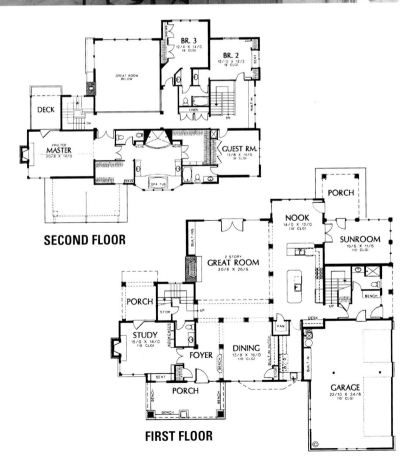

SECOND FLOOR

FIRST FLOOR

Design 91595

Price Code	L
Total Finished	4,768 sq. ft.
First Finished	2,597 sq. ft.
Second Finished	2,171 sq. ft.
Dimensions	76'6"x68'6"
Foundation	Crawlspace
Bedrooms	4
Full Baths	3
3/4 Baths	1
Half Baths	1

Please note: The photographed home may have been modified to suit homeowner preferences. If you order plans, you may wish to have a builder or design professional check them against the photographs to confirm construction details.

living LARGE

above The two-story recessed entryway and the trio of soaring gables are the focal points of this large home's front facade.

High ceilings, big rooms, and lots of natural light add up to large-scale living in this spacious contemporary home. Shared spaces include a nearly 340-square-foot great room with fireplace, media center, vaulted ceiling, and French doors onto a rear grilling porch. A 375-square-foot master bedroom dominates a secluded wing of the house. Off the master bedroom is the spacious master bath, which spreads out under a vaulted ceiling to encompass more than 300 square feet within which are two widely separated vanities, a glass shower enclosure, whirlpool tub, and water closet. Adjoining the master bath is a large walk-in closet.

Upstairs are four secondary bedrooms, each generously sized, and three full baths. Also upstairs is a large attic storage area and behind that a big bonus space, which could some day be finished to become a home office, playroom, or media room. This home is designed with slab and crawlspace foundation options. 🏛

below With its two-story height, the great room in this home is big enough and versatile enough to hold large parties or intimate gatherings.

PHOTOGRAPHY: COURTESY OF THE DESIGNER

left A center island, which holds a prep sink, provides seating space for about four chairs. Behind the wall to the right are the laundry room and walk-in pantry.

below Lots of natural light pours into the sunny breakfast area, which opens onto the rear porch to expand dining options.

Design 62082

Price Code	L
Total Finished	4,461 sq. ft.
First Finished	2,861 sq. ft.
Second Finished	1,600 sq. ft.
Bonus Unfinished	250 sq. ft.
Garage Unfinished	610 sq. ft.
Dimensions	79'10"x60'6"
Foundation	Crawlspace
	Slab
Bedrooms	5
Full Baths	3
3/4 Baths	1
Half Baths	1

Please note: The photographed home may have been modified to suit homeowner preferences. If you order plans, you may wish to have a builder or design professional check them against the photographs to confirm construction details.

FIRST FLOOR

SECOND FLOOR

creating AN OLD HOUSE

We have a funny relationship with old houses. We love the way they look and the way they make us feel. Yet their floorplans are chopped up and parceled into impractical parts. Chris Baldwin, an Illinois designer/builder, wanted the best of old and new. He wanted the warmth and charm of an old farmhouse with all the spaces that a modern family needs. And this is what he came up with: a "Carpenter Gothic farmhouse."

The porch posts, cornices, and latticework look genuine. The large gable over the porch, with its distinctive crossed millwork, the two styles of dormers, and the massive chimney all say that this is the real thing.

Inside, however, the house is not quite so traditional. First, there's what the designer calls "the quarter-round room," a breakfast nook that's just off the family room. And throughout the rest of the house, Baldwin designed in other little surprises, like the octagonal towers. The front tower holds the dining room on the main level and a bedroom upstairs. The rear tower houses the family room downstairs and, upstairs, part of the master suite.

The home's large, open floor plan includes a huge media room and three-car garage. This home is designed with a basement foundation. 🏛

above Details such as the heavy chimney, gable with millwork, and porch with lattice all contribute to a feeling of true authenticity in this Carpenter Gothic style home.

below This small library was carved out of the front gable of the house. The addition of exposed rafters, custom bookcases, and a library ladder make this landing space something special.

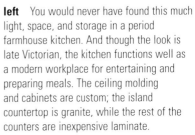

left You would never have found this much light, space, and storage in a period farmhouse kitchen. And though the look is late Victorian, the kitchen functions well as a modern workplace for entertaining and preparing meals. The ceiling molding and cabinets are custom; the island countertop is granite, while the rest of the counters are inexpensive laminate.

below Heavy crown and picture molding and period window trim, all set off by the deep red walls and ceiling, contribute to the warmth and traditional feel of the living room.

Design 19182

Price Code	L
Total Finished	4,823 sq. ft.
First Finished	2,050 sq. ft.
Second Finished	2,773 sq. ft.
Basement Unfinished	2,050 sq. ft.
Garage Unfinished	816 sq. ft.
Dimensions	65'x81'
Foundation	Basement
Bedrooms	4
Full Baths	3
Half Baths	2

Please note: The photographed home may have been modified to suit homeowner preferences. If you order plans, you may wish to have a builder or design professional check them against the photographs to confirm construction details.

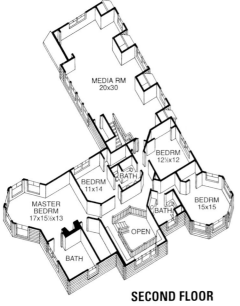

SECOND FLOOR

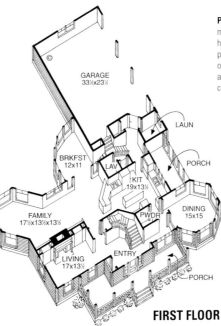

FIRST FLOOR

single-level LUXURY

At over 2,200 square feet, this home offers single-level luxury that's complete in every respect. With its elegant window details, large kitchen with attached breakfast area, three bedrooms, and three-car garage, this traditionally designed home is magnificently designed for maximum livability and practical function.

The bedrooms are set apart from the common areas, creating a strong definition of private and public. The living room, kitchen, and breakfast nook blend into each other, promoting a family-friendly atmosphere. And while closets abound through both areas, a large utility room allows for even more storage space. This home is designed with a slab foundation. 🏛

above Graceful gables accent the front entry, which is accompanied by a small, elegant porch. To the right is a discrete three-car garage.

below An elegant column separates the large living room from the foyer and formal dining room. The doorway in the center of the photo leads to the bedroom wing of the home.

PHOTOGRAPHY: CHRIS A. LITTLE

above & below A quiet, sun-filled corner of the kitchen is given over to the breakfast nook, just right for quiet family meals. The angled breakfast bar provides plenty of extra work space while keeping the room light and open. For more formal occasions, there's the dining room toward the front of the home.

Please note: The photographed home may have been modified to suit homeowner preferences. If you order plans, you may wish to have a builder or design professional check them against the photographs to confirm construction details.

Design 94676

Price Code	D
Total Finished	2,201 sq. ft.
Main Finished	2,201 sq. ft.
Garage Unfinished	853 sq. ft.
Deck Unfinished	222 sq. ft.
Porch Unfinished	240 sq. ft.
Dimensions	71'10"x66'10"
Foundation	Slab
Bedrooms	3
Full Baths	2
Half Baths	1

MAIN FLOOR

sinks for CHEFS

above   Here's something new and unusual: a sink/cook center combination. Made of 18-gauge stainless steel, it includes a standard sink plus an integrated cooking vessel for steaming, boiling, poaching and blanching.
(Photo courtesy of Kohler Co.)

Our parents had relatively few choices when it came to choosing a kitchen sink: enameled steel, cast-iron, or stainless steel. Today the choices are so varied that they're nearly overwhelming, and you don't just choose the material, but also its style, type, color, and bowl configuration.

Also, the sink you choose today must accommodate the type of faucet you want, plus add-ons like sprayers and soap dispensers, all of which require enough cutouts to accommodate the accessories.

Depending on your budget and your taste, a new kitchen sink can cost anywhere from $50 to several thousand dollars. For instance, a low-end home center stainless-steel model can be yours for about $50, whereas a high-end stainless sink can cost more than $1,600. Get into more exotic materials, and the cost can go even higher. A one-of-a-kind hand-made copper sink (a double bowl with backsplash) from Dino Rachiele can cost about $4,000. A German Silver Sink Co. fixture can run $4,200 or more.

What's Out There
Odds are, you're not in the market for a kitchen sink that costs as much as a semester in college. If you're like most homeowners, you want something that holds up to heavy use, looks good, is easy to maintain, and won't cost you a small fortune. Fortunately, there are lots of good sinks out there that fit several or all of those criteria.

above   This two-bowl undermount stainless-steel sink is one of the most popular sink types installed in new homes today. Good stainless steel, such as this 18-gauge stainless, resists dents and staining, and its heavy undercoating reduces noise. (Photo courtesy of Kohler Co.)

Stainless Steel:
Stick with High Quality

If put to a vote, stainless steel sinks would likely top the popularity list, followed by solid surface (Corian, etc.) and composite sinks, with cast-iron coming in third. The reason that stainless sinks are so popular is that they're affordable, durable, and work well when mounted under the countertop (called an under-mount sink).

Bryan Farrow, with Kitchen Designers Inc. in Marietta, Georgia, says his clients use undermounted stainless steel sinks "because the majority of countertops are granite and most people are using stainless steel undermount sinks because you need the rim strength. Everything's held to the countertop by the rim. Most of the inexpensive sinks don't even come as undermounts."

When choosing a stainless steel sink, look for the highest-grade stainless, which is known as Type 302 (18/8). This kind of steel contains 18% chromium and 8% nickel for a really durable, rust-resistant finish. Also, look at the gauge, or thickness, of the stainless steel sink, because a thicker sink is less likely to dent than a thinner sink, plus the thicker sink won't be as noisy as the thinner, tinnier one. Just remember that the lower the gauge number, the thicker the steel. While most sinks come in 18- to 20-gauge, sinks in 14- and 16-gauge steel are available on the high end, as well as 24-gauge on the lower end.

A satin or brushed finish seems to be the current most popular finish for sinks. Besides being popular, the brushed finish makes the sink easier to clean than glossy finishes, which tend to spot.

Although older stainless sinks were quite noisy, improvements in sound deadening technology have virtually eliminated this problem. Now, all but very low-end stainless steel sinks are sold with a factory applied undercoating that reduces the sound of pots, pans, dishes and silverware banging against the sides of the bowl.

Solid Surface:
The Seamless Material

In popularity, solid surface sinks rank in second place. And when it comes to solid surface materials, most people think of DuPont's Corian, which is the oldest (having debuted in 1969) of the non-porous, acrylic brands used in countertops and integral sinks. Other manufacturers of solid surface sinks include Gibraltar, Avonite, Surell, Swanstone, Fountainhead, and Wilsonart.

A huge benefit of an integral solid surface sink is that it's seamlessly joined to the solid surface countertop, which means no little crevices to collect moisture and grime build-up.

Amy Sussek, a kitchen

above   The beauty of a solid-surface sink is that it's fused with the solid-surface countertop to form one seamless piece, which means easy cleanup and low maintenance. (Photo courtesy of Corian)

above This classic two-bowl cast-iron sink comes from the factory with an unsurpassed gleaming finish and a deep, rich color. When choosing cast-iron, don't skimp; buy from a quality manufacturer. (Photo courtesy Kohler Co.)

designer and a host of AsktheKitchenDesigner.com, suggests to her clients that, if they want a solid surface countertop with an under-mounted sink, they get an integral solid surface sink as well.

"If you do use an undermount sink, the [solid surface] fabricator charges a couple hundred dollars to do the sink cutout, then you still have the price of the sink to consider," according to Sussek. "If it's an integral sink (basically a one-piece, solid-surface sink-countertop combination), you don't have that extra cost, just the cost of the sink added to the cost of the counter."

Cast-iron: The Heavy Standard

A perennial kitchen favorite going back to the 19th century is the porcelain-coated cast-iron sink. Although it's still a great value, it's mostly relegated to use in kitchens that use laminate or some other type of countertop that requires a so-called drop-in sink (as opposed to one that is undermounted or surface-mounted).

Cast-iron has its critics. Some complain that the porcelain coating on modern cast-iron sinks chips more easily than it used to. But, the porcelain coating will chip on even the best and most expensive cast-iron sink if you're not careful—just like a Rolls Royce will dent if you carelessly back it over the neighbor's mailbox.

Both kitchen designers and plumbers recommend that you stick with name-brand manufacturers when you buy a cast-iron sink. And before it's installed, make sure to check it for chips, especially around the rim, which can rust.

What Else Is Out There?

From high end to low end, the world is full of other types of sinks. At the least-expensive level, there are enameled steel sinks, which, thanks to heavy spray-on undercoatings, perform much like cast-iron sinks but at a much lower price.

Composite sinks are another type on the market that are giving the solid surface sinks a run for their money. Composites are often made from quartz or granite mixed with an acrylic binder. These sinks are fairly hard, scratch resistant, and good values for the money.

below Relatively new on the scene are so-called composite sinks like this undermount sink made of Silacron, which is 70% quartz making it very resistant to scratches and stains as well as heat resistant up to 446 degrees. This model includes a waste-chute system accessory, a large bowl, and a smaller prep-sink bowl. (Photo compliments of Blanco America)

On the high end are a gamut of sink types from fireclay to, believe it or not, carved granite. It's probably unnecessary to remind you of this, but anything out of the ordinary-especially anything hand made or created custom or in small quantities-costs more than the mass-produced sinks you'll find at home centers and kitchen and bath shops.

Margaret Clarkson, a kitchen designer at Walker Zanger, Inc. in Atlanta, sells an imported farmhouse sink that's carved from a solid block of limestone. "Our business is tile and stone," she said. "And this sink, which retails for $2,400, is absolutely beautiful—it's 17 inches by 29 inches by 11 inches deep."

Other high-end types of kitchen sinks include marble, soapstone, copper, and German silver (which is a copper), nickel, and zinc composite.

One of the more popular, and at the same time traditional, high-end sinks is soapstone, which is created by joining slabs of soapstone with epoxy to form the sink basin. One complaint about soapstone is that the bottom of the sink is so perfectly flat that anything on the bottom of the sink, like crumbs, must be manually swept toward the drain. Otherwise, it's a beautiful material and ages gracefully.

Fireclay sinks, which have probably been around longer than even cast-iron, are one of the newest trends in kitchen fixtures. Made by pouring liquid

above   This high end farmhouse sink was carved from a single block of limestone. The manufacturer recommends that all stone sinks (or natural stone tiles and countertops) be sealed with a penetrating sealer. Even then, acidic liquids such as lemon juice or vinegar may etch the stone surface. (Photo compliments Walker Zanger)

clay into a mold, then removed from the mold and sponged to a slick finish, fireclay sinks are then allowed to air dry. Later they're sprayed with a ceramic finish and fired in a kiln. Fireclay is very hard and durable and reportedly doesn't chip nearly as easily as cast-iron. It can be pricey though, costing hundreds of dollars or more depending on the finish and any decoration.

Keep in mind as you make your decision, that many of these high-end sinks require wall-mounted faucets, which are expensive and often hard to find in just the style you want for your kitchen. ⬚

Design 10515

See Order Pages and Index for Info

PHOTOGRAPHY: JOHN EHRENCLOU

Units	Single
Price Code	D
Total Finished	2,015 sq. ft.
First Finished	1,280 sq. ft.
Second Finished	735 sq. ft.
Porch Unfinished	80 sq. ft.
Dimensions	32'x40'
Foundation	Crawlspace
Bedrooms	3
Full Baths	2
Half Baths	I
First Ceiling	8'
Second Ceiling	8'
Max Ridge Height	32'
Roof Framing	Stick
Exterior Walls	2x6

Please note: The photographed home may have been modified to suit homeowner preferences. If you order plans, have a builder or design professional check them against the photograph to confirm actual construction details.

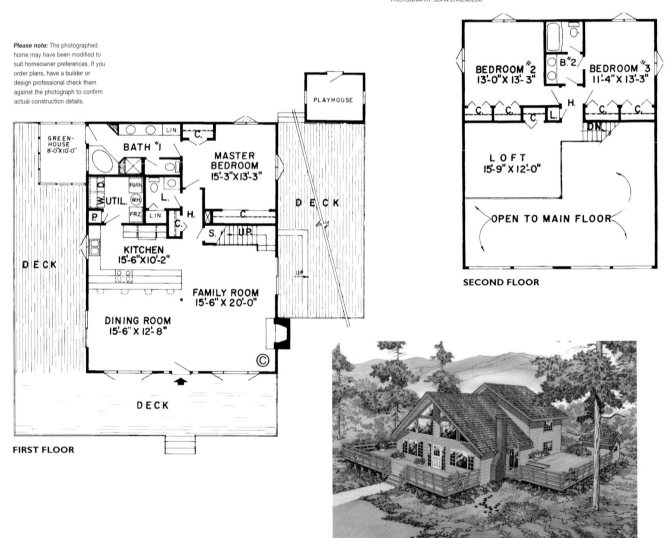

FIRST FLOOR

PLAYHOUSE

GREEN-HOUSE
8'-0"X10'-0"

BATH #1

LIN.
C.

MASTER BEDROOM
15'-3"X13'-3"

DECK

FURN

WD

UTIL.

WH

P

FRZ

LIN

H.
C.

KITCHEN
15'-6"X10'-2"

S.   UP

UP

DECK

FAMILY ROOM
15'-6" X 20'-0"

DINING ROOM
15'-6" X 12'-8"

DECK

SECOND FLOOR

BEDROOM #2
13'-0" X 13'-3"

B. #2

BEDROOM #3
11'-4" X 13'-3"

C.   C.   C.   L.   H.   C.   C.

LOFT
15'-9" X 12'-0"

DN

OPEN TO MAIN FLOOR

FRONT & SIDE ELEVATION

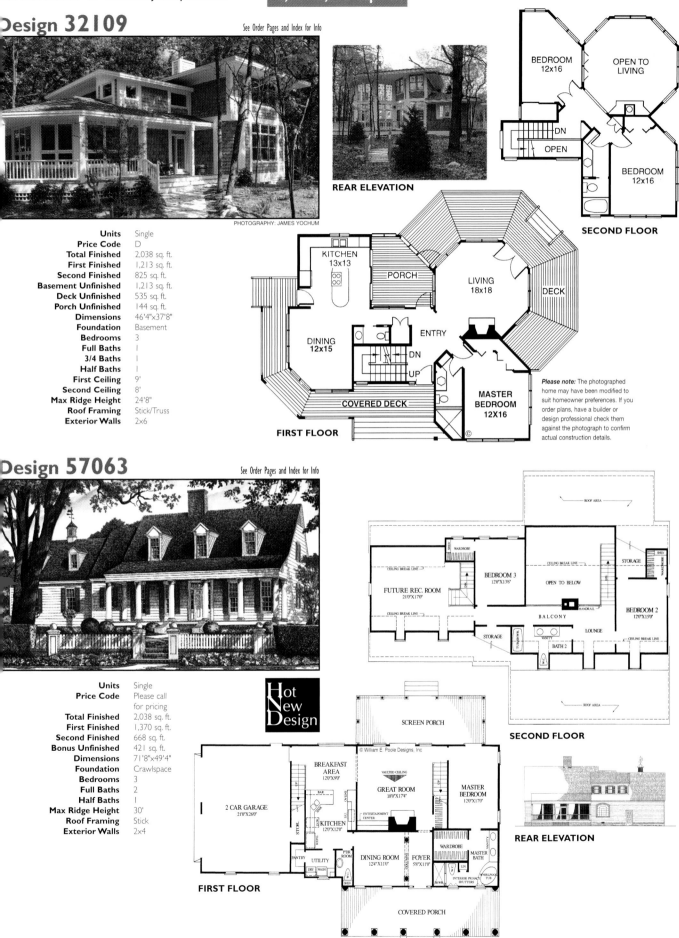

Design 32109

See Order Pages and Index for Info

REAR ELEVATION

PHOTOGRAPHY: JAMES YOCHUM

Units	Single
Price Code	D
Total Finished	2,038 sq. ft.
First Finished	1,213 sq. ft.
Second Finished	825 sq. ft.
Basement Unfinished	1,213 sq. ft.
Deck Unfinished	535 sq. ft.
Porch Unfinished	144 sq. ft.
Dimensions	46'4"x37'8"
Foundation	Basement
Bedrooms	3
Full Baths	1
3/4 Baths	1
Half Baths	1
First Ceiling	9'
Second Ceiling	8'
Max Ridge Height	24'8"
Roof Framing	Stick/Truss
Exterior Walls	2x6

SECOND FLOOR

BEDROOM 12x16 / OPEN TO LIVING / BEDROOM 12x16

FIRST FLOOR

KITCHEN 13x13 / PORCH / LIVING 18x18 / DECK / DINING 12x15 / ENTRY / MASTER BEDROOM 12X16 / COVERED DECK

Please note: The photographed home may have been modified to suit homeowner preferences. If you order plans, have a builder or design professional check them against the photograph to confirm actual construction details.

Design 57063

See Order Pages and Index for Info

Hot New Design

Units	Single
Price Code	Please call for pricing
Total Finished	2,038 sq. ft.
First Finished	1,370 sq. ft.
Second Finished	668 sq. ft.
Bonus Unfinished	421 sq. ft.
Dimensions	71'8"x49'4"
Foundation	Crawlspace
Bedrooms	3
Full Baths	2
Half Baths	1
Max Ridge Height	30'
Roof Framing	Stick
Exterior Walls	2x4

SECOND FLOOR

FUTURE REC. ROOM / BEDROOM 3 / OPEN TO BELOW / STORAGE / BEDROOM 2 / BALCONY / LOUNGE / BATH 2

© William E. Poole Designs, Inc

FIRST FLOOR

2 CAR GARAGE / BREAKFAST AREA / GREAT ROOM / MASTER BEDROOM / KITCHEN / ENTERTAINMENT CENTER / DINING ROOM / FOYER / MASTER BATH / SCREEN PORCH / COVERED PORCH

REAR ELEVATION

Design 98427

See Order Pages and Index for Info

Units	Single
Price Code	D
Total Finished	2,051 sq. ft.
Main Finished	2,051 sq. ft.
Basement Unfinished	2,051 sq. ft.
Garage Unfinished	441 sq. ft.
Dimensions	56'x60'6"
Foundation	Basement
	Crawlspace
	Slab
Bedrooms	3
Full Baths	2
Main Ceiling	9'
Max Ridge Height	27'5"
Roof Framing	Stick
Exterior Walls	2x4

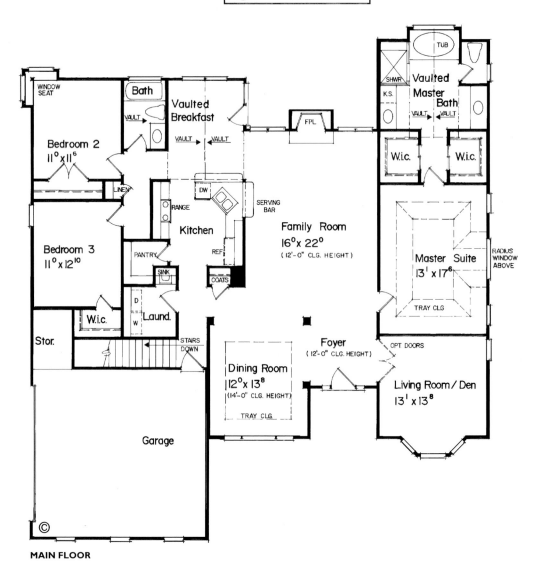

MAIN FLOOR

Design 94260

See Order Pages and Index for Info

Units	Single
Price Code	F
Total Finished	2,068 sq. ft.
Main Finished	2,068 sq. ft.
Basement Unfinished	1,402 sq. ft.
Garage Unfinished	560 sq. ft.
Deck Unfinished	594 sq. ft.
Porch Unfinished	696 sq. ft.
Dimensions	54'x58'
Foundation	Pier/Post
Bedrooms	3
Full Baths	2
Max Ridge Height	37'
Roof Framing	Truss
Exterior Walls	2x6

* Alternate foundation options available at an additional charge.
Please call 1-800-235-5700 for more information.

REAR ELEVATION

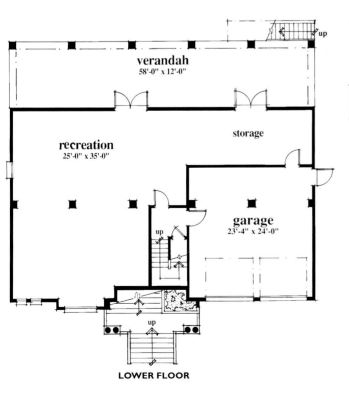

LOWER FLOOR

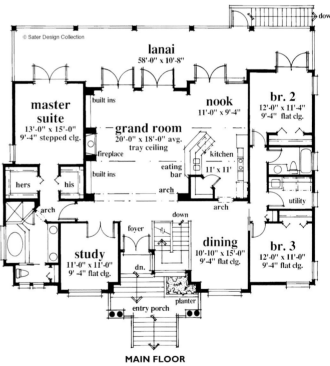

MAIN FLOOR

See thousands more plans at www.familyhomeplans.com

2,001-2,500 Sq. Ft.

Design 96505

See Order Pages and Index for Info

Units	Single
Price Code	D
Total Finished	2,069 sq. ft.
Main Finished	2,069 sq. ft.
Garage Unfinished	481 sq. ft.
Porch Unfinished	374 sq. ft.
Dimensions	70'x58'
Foundation	Crawlspace
	Slab
Bedrooms	3
Full Baths	2
Half Baths	1
Main Ceiling	9'
Max Ridge Height	23'
Exterior Walls	2x4

MAIN FLOOR

Design 57000

See Order Pages and Index for Info

Units	Single
Price Code	Please call
	for pricing
Total Finished	2,076 sq. ft.
First Finished	1,540 sq. ft.
Second Finished	536 sq. ft.
Bonus Unfinished	502 sq. ft.
Dimensions	62'8"x61'
Foundation	Basement
Bedrooms	3
Full Baths	2
Half Baths	1
Max Ridge Height	24'
Roof Framing	Stick
Exterior Walls	2x4

SECOND FLOOR

FIRST FLOOR

DESIGN 92642

See Order Pages and Index for Info

PHOTOGRAPHY: COURTESY OF THE DESIGNER

Units	Single
Price Code	D
Total Finished	2,082 sq. ft.
First Finished	1,524 sq. ft.
Second Finished	558 sq. ft.
Bonus Unfinished	267 sq. ft.
Basement Unfinished	1,460 sq. ft.
Dimensions	60'×50'4"
Foundation	Basement
Bedrooms	3
Full Baths	2
Half Baths	1
First Ceiling	8'
Second Ceiling	8'
Max Ridge Height	26'
Roof Framing	Truss
Exterior Walls	2×4

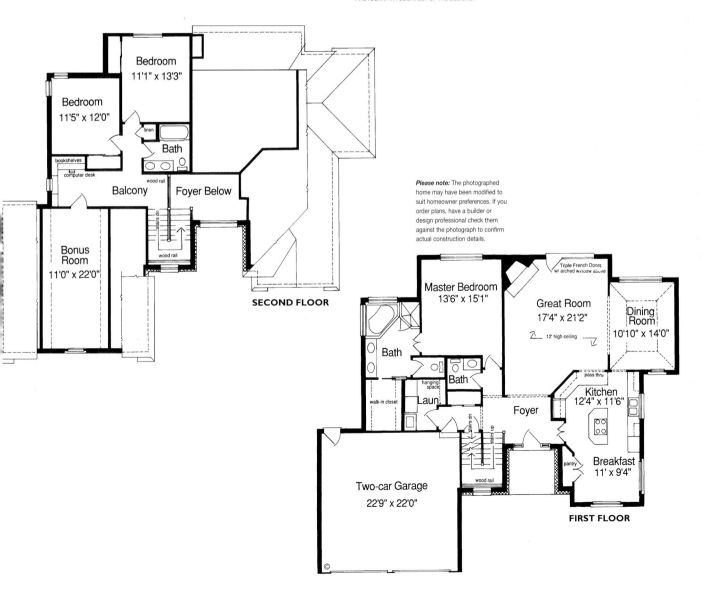

Please note: The photographed home may have been modified to suit homeowner preferences. If you order plans, have a builder or design professional check them against the photograph to confirm actual construction details.

Design 57094

See Order Pages and Index for Info

Units	Single
Price Code	Please call for pricing
Total Finished	2,096 sq. ft.
Main Finished	2,096 sq. ft.
Bonus Unfinished	374 sq. ft.
Dimensions	64'8"x60'
Foundation	Crawlspace
Bedrooms	3
Full Baths	2
Max Ridge Height	29'
Roof Framing	Stick
Exterior Walls	2x4

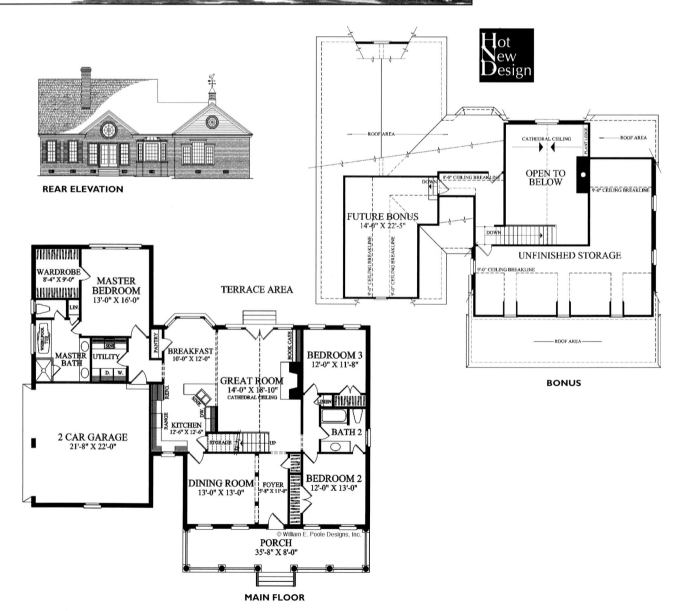

REAR ELEVATION

Hot New Design

FUTURE BONUS
14'-0" X 22'-5"

OPEN TO BELOW

CATHEDRAL CEILING

ROOF AREA

8'-0" CEILING BREAKLINE

9'-0" CEILING BREAKLINE

DOWN

UNFINISHED STORAGE

9'-0" CEILING BREAKLINE

ROOF AREA

BONUS

WARDROBE
8'-4" X 9'-0"

MASTER BEDROOM
13'-0" X 16'-0"

TERRACE AREA

LIN.

WHIRLPOOL TUB

MASTER BATH

SINK

UTILITY

D. W.

PANTRY

BREAKFAST
10'-0" X 12'-0"

BOOK CASE

BEDROOM 3
12'-0" X 11'-8"

GREAT ROOM
14'-0" X 18'-10"
CATHEDRAL CEILING

REFG.

RANGE

SINK

DW

LINEN

KITCHEN
12'-6" X 12'-6"

STORAGE

UP

BATH 2

2 CAR GARAGE
21'-8" X 22'-0"

DINING ROOM
13'-0" X 13'-0"

FOYER
9'-8" X 11'-0"

BEDROOM 2
12'-0" X 13'-0"

© William E. Poole Designs, Inc.

PORCH
35'-8" X 8'-0"

MAIN FLOOR

Design 96529

See Order Pages and Index for Info

Units	Single
Price Code	D
Total Finished	2,089 sq. ft.
Main Finished	2,089 sq. ft.
Bonus Unfinished	497 sq. ft.
Garage Unfinished	541 sq. ft.
Dimensions	79'x52'
Foundation	Crawlspace
	Slab
Bedrooms	3
Full Baths	2
Half Baths	1
Main Ceiling	9'
Max Ridge Height	22'
Roof Framing	Stick
Exterior Walls	2x4

BONUS

MAIN FLOOR

Design 93212

See Order Pages and Index for Info

Units	Single
Price Code	D
Total Finished	2,091 sq. ft.
First Finished	1,362 sq. ft.
Second Finished	729 sq. ft.
Bonus Unfinished	384 sq. ft.
Basement Unfinished	988 sq. ft.
Garage Unfinished	559 sq. ft.
Porch Unfinished	396 sq. ft.
Dimensions	78'x38'
Foundation	Basement
	Crawlspace
	Slab
Bedrooms	3
Full Baths	2
Half Baths	1
Max Ridge Height	23'
Roof Framing	Stick
Exterior Walls	2x4

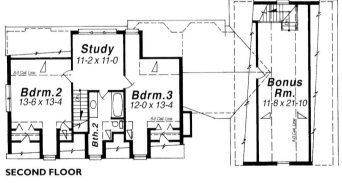

SECOND FLOOR

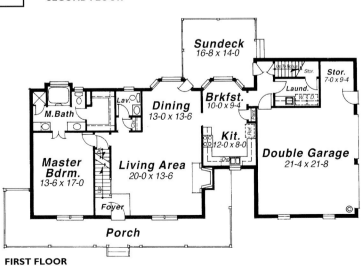

FIRST FLOOR

Design 92610

See Order Pages and Index for Info

PHOTOGRAPHY: DONNA & RON KOLB, EXPOSURES UMLIMITED

Units	Single
Price Code	D
Total Finished	2,101 sq. ft.
First Finished	1,626 sq. ft.
Second Finished	475 sq. ft.
Basement Unfinished	1,512 sq. ft.
Garage Unfinished	438 sq. ft.
Dimensions	59'x60'8"
Foundation	Basement
Bedrooms	3
Full Baths	2
Half Baths	I
First Ceiling	8'
Second Ceiling	8'
Max Ridge Height	31'
Roof Framing	Truss
Exterior Walls	2x4

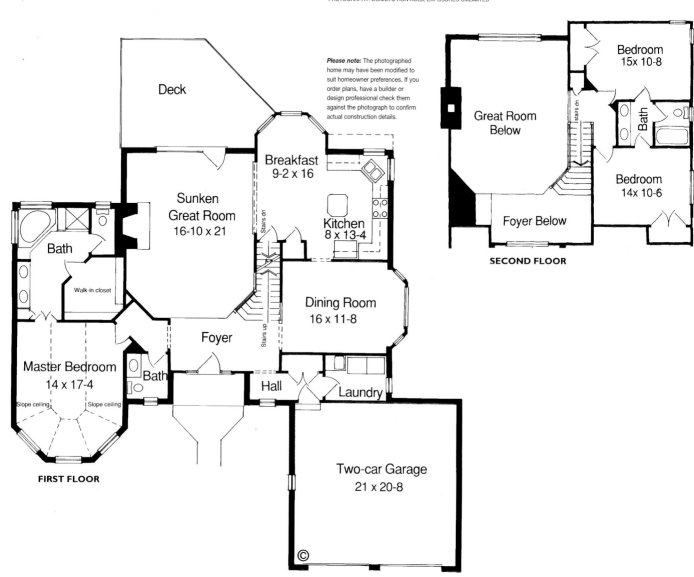

Please note: The photographed home may have been modified to suit homeowner preferences. If you order plans, have a builder or design professional check them against the photograph to confirm actual construction details.

FIRST FLOOR

SECOND FLOOR

Design 97219

See Order Pages and Index for Info

Units	Single
Price Code	D
Total Finished	2,128 sq. ft.
First Finished	1,257 sq. ft.
Second Finished	871 sq. ft.
Bonus Unfinished	444 sq. ft.
Basement Unfinished	1,275 sq. ft.
Garage Unfinished	462 sq. ft.
Dimensions	61'x40'6"
Foundation	Basement Crawlspace
Bedrooms	4
Full Baths	3
Half Baths	1
Max Ridge Height	32'
Roof Framing	Stick
Exterior Walls	2x4

CAD FILES AVAILABLE
For more information call
800-235-5700

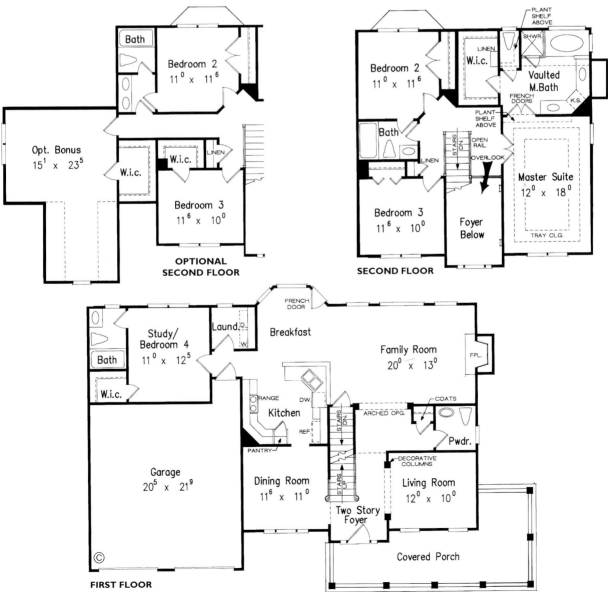

OPTIONAL SECOND FLOOR

Bath

Bedroom 2
11⁰ x 11⁶

Opt. Bonus
15¹ x 23⁵

W.i.c.

W.i.c.

LINEN

Bedroom 3
11⁶ x 10⁰

SECOND FLOOR

PLANT SHELF ABOVE

SHWR

LINEN

W.i.c.

Bedroom 2
11⁰ x 11⁶

Vaulted M.Bath

FRENCH DOORS

K.S.

Bath

PLANT SHELF ABOVE

OPEN RAIL

OVERLOOK

STAIRS DN.

Master Suite
12⁰ x 18⁰

LINEN

Bedroom 3
11⁶ x 10⁰

Foyer Below

TRAY CLG.

FIRST FLOOR

FRENCH DOOR

Study/ Bedroom 4
11⁰ x 12⁵

Laund.

Breakfast

Family Room
20⁰ x 13⁰

FPL.

Bath

W.i.c.

RANGE

Kitchen

DW.

REF.

COATS

ARCHED OPG.

STAIRS DN.

Pwdr.

Garage
20⁵ x 21⁹

PANTRY

DECORATIVE COLUMNS

Dining Room
11⁶ x 11⁰

STAIRS UP

Two Story Foyer

Living Room
12⁰ x 10⁰

Covered Porch

2,001-2,500 Sq. Ft.

Design 20179

See Order Pages and Index for Info

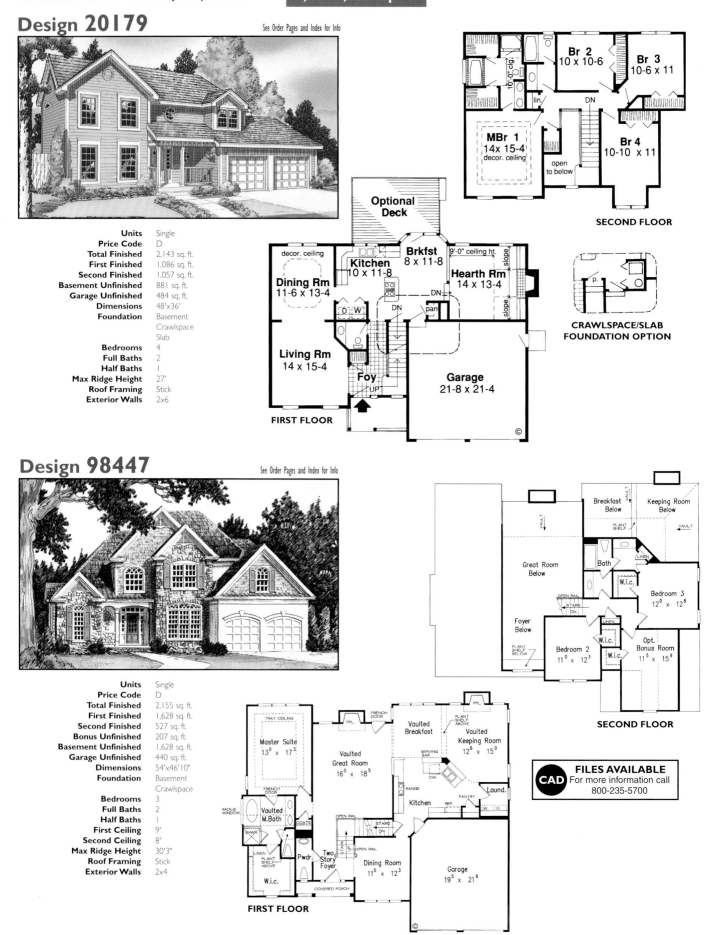

Units	Single
Price Code	D
Total Finished	2,143 sq. ft.
First Finished	1,086 sq. ft.
Second Finished	1,057 sq. ft.
Basement Unfinished	881 sq. ft.
Garage Unfinished	484 sq. ft.
Dimensions	48'x36'
Foundation	Basement
	Crawlspace
	Slab
Bedrooms	4
Full Baths	2
Half Baths	1
Max Ridge Height	27'
Roof Framing	Stick
Exterior Walls	2x6

SECOND FLOOR

Br 2 10 x 10-6
Br 3 10-6 x 11
MBr 1 14x 15-4 decor. ceiling
Br 4 10-10 x 11
DN
open to below
10'-0" clg.
lin

CRAWLSPACE/SLAB FOUNDATION OPTION

Optional Deck

Kitchen 10 x 11-8
Brkfst 8 x 11-8
9'-0" ceiling ht.
decor. ceiling
Dining Rm 11-6 x 13-4
Hearth Rm 14 x 13-4
slope
DN
DN
pan
Living Rm 14 x 15-4
Garage 21-8 x 21-4
Foy
UP

FIRST FLOOR

Design 98447

See Order Pages and Index for Info

Units	Single
Price Code	D
Total Finished	2,155 sq. ft.
First Finished	1,628 sq. ft.
Second Finished	527 sq. ft.
Bonus Unfinished	207 sq. ft.
Basement Unfinished	1,628 sq. ft.
Garage Unfinished	440 sq. ft.
Dimensions	54'x46'10"
Foundation	Basement
	Crawlspace
Bedrooms	3
Full Baths	2
Half Baths	1
First Ceiling	9'
Second Ceiling	8'
Max Ridge Height	30'3"
Roof Framing	Stick
Exterior Walls	2x4

SECOND FLOOR

Breakfast Below
Keeping Room Below
VAULT
PLANT SHELF
LINEN
Great Room Below
Bath
W.i.c.
Bedroom 3 12⁰ x 12⁸
OPEN RAIL STAIRS DN
Foyer Below
LINEN
W.i.c.
PLANT SHELF BELOW
Bedroom 2 11⁰ x 12³
W.i.c.
Opt. Bonus Room 11⁵ x 15⁹

FILES AVAILABLE
For more information call 800-235-5700

TRAY CEILING
Master Suite 13⁰ x 17³
FRENCH DOOR
FPL
FRENCH DOOR
Vaulted Breakfast
PLANT SHELF ABOVE
FPL
Vaulted Keeping Room 12⁶ x 15⁰
Vaulted Great Room 16⁰ x 18⁵
SERVING BAR
DW.
RANGE
Kitchen
PANTRY
REF.
Laund.
W. D.
RADIUS WINDOW
Vaulted M.Bath
COATS
SHWR
LINEN
PLANT SHELF ABOVE
Pwdr.
Two Story Foyer
OPEN RAIL
STAIRS DN
OPEN RAIL
Dining Room 11⁰ x 12³
Garage 19⁵ x 21⁹
W.i.c.
COVERED PORCH

FIRST FLOOR

Design 19410

See Order Pages and Index for Info

Units	Single
Price Code	D
Total Finished	2,175 sq. ft.
First Finished	1,600 sq. ft.
Second Finished	575 sq. ft.
Basement Unfinished	1,509 sq. ft.
Garage Unfinished	413 sq. ft.
Dimensions	48'4"x60'
Foundation	Basement
Bedrooms	4
Full Baths	2
Half Baths	1
First Ceiling	8'4"
Second Ceiling	8'4"
Roof Framing	Stick
Exterior Walls	2x4

PHOTOGRAPHY: MIKE MORELAND

Please note: The photographed home may have been modified to suit homeowner preferences. If you order plans, have a builder or design professional check them against the photograph to confirm actual construction details.

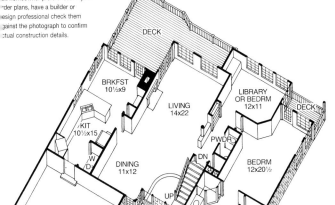

FIRST FLOOR

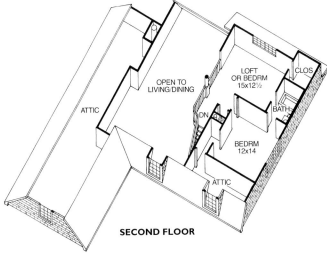

SECOND FLOOR

UNFINISHED BASEMENT

REAR ELEVATION

Design 98466

See Order Pages and Index for Info

Units	Single
Price Code	D
Total Finished	2,193 sq. ft.
Main Finished	2,193 sq. ft.
Bonus Unfinished	400 sq. ft.
Basement Unfinished	2,193 sq. ft.
Garage Unfinished	522 sq. ft.
Dimensions	64'6"x59'
Foundation	Basement
	Crawlspace
	Slab
Bedrooms	4
Full Baths	2
Main Ceiling	9'
Second Ceiling	8'
Max Ridge Height	27'
Roof Framing	Stick
Exterior Walls	2x4

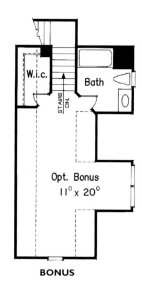

BONUS

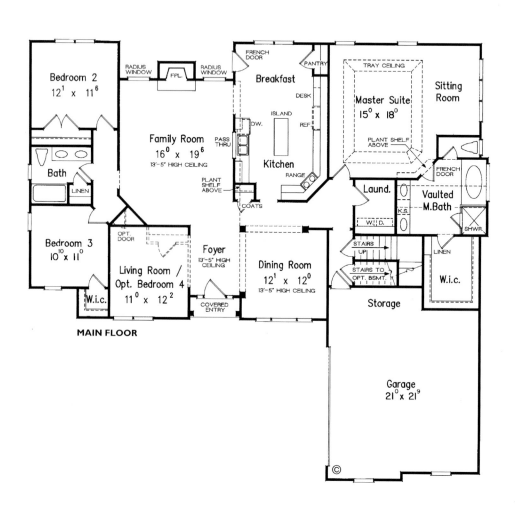

MAIN FLOOR

Design 90454

See Order Pages and Index for Info

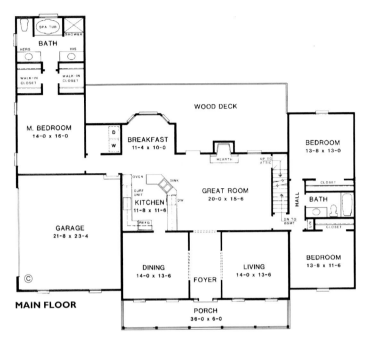

Units	Single
Price Code	D
Total Finished	2,218 sq. ft.
Main Finished	2,218 sq. ft.
Basement Unfinished	1,658 sq. ft.
Garage Unfinished	528 sq. ft.
Deck Unfinished	342 sq. ft.
Porch Unfinished	216 sq. ft.
Dimensions	72'x64'
Foundation	Basement
	Crawlspace
Bedrooms	3
Full Baths	2
Main Ceiling	9'
Max Ridge Height	20'10"
Roof Framing	Stick
Exterior Walls	2x4

MAIN FLOOR

Design 65138

See Order Pages and Index for Info

PHOTOGRAPHY: COURTESY OF THE DESIGNER

Units	Single
Price Code	D
Total Finished	2,257 sq. ft.
First Finished	1,274 sq. ft.
Second Finished	983 sq. ft.
Garage Unfinished	437 sq. ft.
Porch Unfinished	183 sq. ft.
Dimensions	50'x46'
Foundation	Basement
Bedrooms	3
Full Baths	2
Half Baths	1
First Ceiling	9'
Second Ceiling	8'
Max Ridge Height	30'11'
Roof Framing	Truss
Exterior Walls	2x6

LIVING ROOM

Please note: The photographed home may have been modified to suit home-owner preferences. If you order plans, have a builder or design professional check them against the photograph to confirm actual construction details.

SECOND FLOOR

FIRST FLOOR

Design 32387

See Order Pages and Index for Info

PHOTOGRAPHY: MICHAEL PARTENIO

Units	Single
Price Code	D
Total Finished	2,241 sq. ft.
First Finished	1,146 sq. ft.
Second Finished	1,095 sq. ft.
Bonus Unfinished	350 sq. ft.
Basement Unfinished	1,138 sq. ft.
Garage Unfinished	457 sq. ft.
Deck Unfinished	126 sq. ft.
Dimensions	54'x45'
Foundation	Basement
Bedrooms	3
Full Baths	2
3/4 Baths	1
First Ceiling	9'
Second Ceiling	8'
Max Ridge Height	35'
Roof Framing	Stick
Exterior Walls	2x6

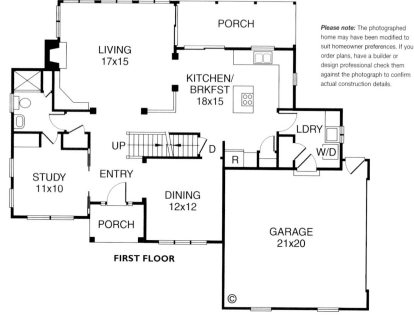

REAR ELEVATION

Please note: The photographed home may have been modified to suit homeowner preferences. If you order plans, have a builder or design professional check them against the photograph to confirm actual construction details.

SECOND FLOOR

MASTER BEDROOM 14x19

BEDROOM 12x13

BATH

BATH

DN

BEDROOM 12x12

BONUS ROOM 16x21

FIRST FLOOR

PORCH

LIVING 17x15

KITCHEN/ BRKFST 18x15

LDRY

W/D

UP   D

R

STUDY 11x10

ENTRY

DINING 12x12

PORCH

GARAGE 21x20

Design 68162

See Order Pages and Index for Info

Units	Single
Price Code	E
Total Finished	2,252 sq. ft.
First Finished	1,736 sq. ft.
Second Finished	516 sq. ft.
Bonus Unfinished	242 sq. ft.
Garage Unfinished	638 sq. ft.
Deck Unfinished	1,223 sq. ft.
Dimensions	80'x59'
Foundation	Slab
Bedrooms	4
Full Baths	3
First Ceiling	9'
Max Ridge Height	30'
Exterior Walls	2x4

* Alternate foundation options available at an additional charge.
Please call 1-800-235-5700 for more information.

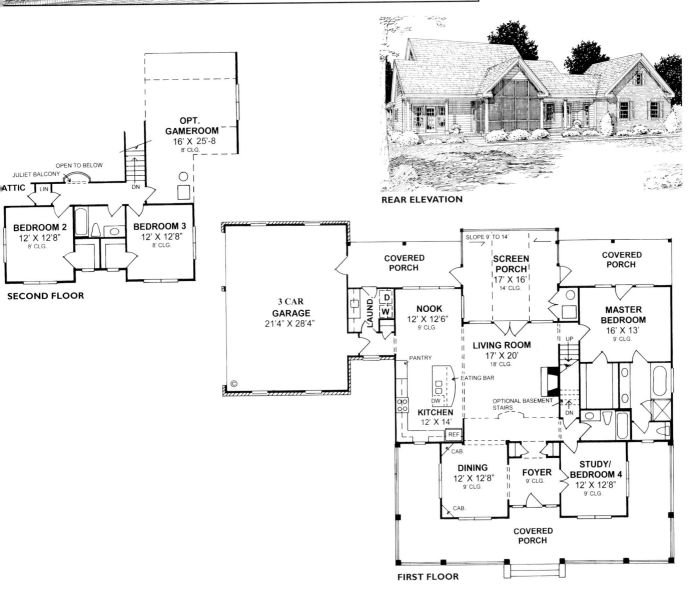

OPT. GAMEROOM
16' X 25'-8
8' CLG.

OPEN TO BELOW

JULIET BALCONY

ATTIC   LIN   DN

BEDROOM 2
12' X 12'8"
8' CLG.

BEDROOM 3
12' X 12'8"
8' CLG.

SECOND FLOOR

REAR ELEVATION

3 CAR GARAGE
21'4" X 28'4"

LAUND.   D W   D W

COVERED PORCH

SLOPE 9' TO 14'

SCREEN PORCH
17' X 16'
14' CLG.

COVERED PORCH

NOOK
12' X 12'6"
9' CLG.

LIVING ROOM
17' X 20'
18' CLG.

MASTER BEDROOM
16' X 13'
9' CLG.

PANTRY

EATING BAR

DW

OPTIONAL BASEMENT STAIRS

UP

DN

KITCHEN
12' X 14'

REF.

CAB.

DINING
12' X 12'8"
9' CLG.

FOYER
9' CLG.

STUDY/ BEDROOM 4
12' X 12'8"
9' CLG.

CAB.

COVERED PORCH

FIRST FLOOR

Design **57080**

See Order Pages and Index for Info

Units	Single
Price Code	Please call for pricing
Total Finished	2,357 sq. ft.
First Finished	1,305 sq. ft.
Second Finished	1,052 sq. ft.
Bonus Unfinished	430 sq. ft.
Dimensions	69'4"x35'10"
Foundation	Crawlspace
Bedrooms	3
Full Baths	2
Half Baths	1
First Ceiling	9'
Roof Framing	Stick

REAR ELEVATION

SECOND FLOOR

FIRST FLOOR

Design 99457

See Order Pages and Index for Info

PHOTOGRAPHY: COURTESY OF THE DESIGNER

Units	Single
Price Code	E
Total Finished	2,270 sq. ft.
First Finished	1,150 sq. ft.
Second Finished	1,120 sq. ft.
Basement Unfinished	1,150 sq. ft.
Garage Unfinished	457 sq. ft.
Dimensions	46'x48'
Foundation	Basement
Bedrooms	4
Full Baths	2
Half Baths	1
First Ceiling	8'
Second Ceiling	8'
Tray Ceiling	9'4"
Max Ridge Height	28'
Roof Framing	Stick
Exterior Walls	2x4

* Alternate foundation options available at an additional charge.
Please call 1-800-235-5700 for more information.

Please note: The photographed home may have been modified to suit homeowner preferences. If you order plans, have a builder or design professional check them against the photograph to confirm actual construction details.

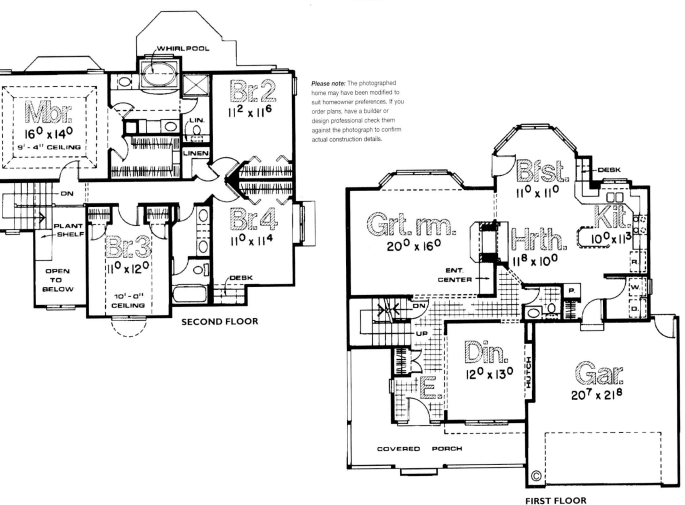

Design **57009**

See Order Pages and Index for Info

© WILLIAM E. POOLE DESIGNS, INC.

Units	Single
Price Code	Please call for pricing
Total Finished	2,272 sq. ft.
First Finished	1,981 sq. ft.
Second Finished	291 sq. ft.
Bonus Unfinished	412 sq. ft.
Dimensions	58'x55'4"
Foundation	Combo Basement/ Crawlspace
Bedrooms	4
Full Baths	3
Half Baths	1
Max Ridge Height	28'
Roof Framing	Stick
Exterior Walls	2x4

Hot New Design

FIRST FLOOR

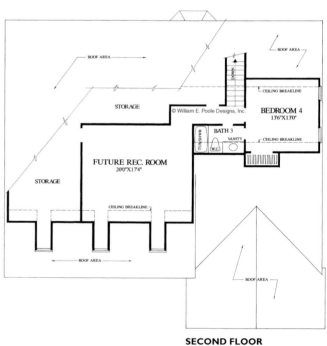

SECOND FLOOR

Design 57072

See Order Pages and Index for Info

Units	Single
Price Code	Please call for pricing
Total Finished	2,253 sq. ft.
First Finished	1,634 sq. ft.
Second Finished	619 sq. ft.
Bonus Unfinished	229 sq. ft.
Dimensions	46'x54'5"
Foundation	Crawlspace
Bedrooms	3
Full Baths	2
Half Baths	1
Max Ridge Height	26'
Roof Framing	Stick
Exterior Walls	2x4

Hot New Design

REAR ELEVATION

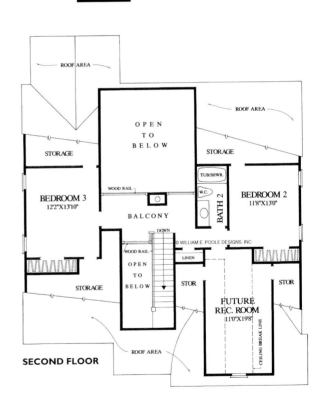

Design 10690

See Order Pages and Index for Info

PHOTOGRAPHY: JOHN EHRENCLOU

Units	Single
Price Code	E
Total Finished	2,281 sq. ft.
First Finished	1,260 sq. ft.
Second Finished	1,021 sq. ft.
Basement Unfinished	1,186 sq. ft.
Garage Unfinished	851 sq. ft.
Dimensions	76'4"x45'10"
Foundation	Basement
	Crawlspace
	Slab
Bedrooms	3
Full Baths	2
Half Baths	1
First Ceiling	9'
Second Ceiling	8'
Vaulted Ceiling	10'
Roof Framing	Stick
Exterior Walls	2x4, 2x6

SECOND FLOOR

- Attic Space (Optional)
- W.P. Tub
- Skylt
- Br #3 — 11-7 x 9-10
- Skylt
- MBr #1 — 12-1 x 15-10 — 8' Clg.
- DN Railing
- Plant Shelf
- Br #2 — 11-7 x 11-10
- Open to Below
- Flat Clg @ 10'
- Lin.

REAR ELEVATION

Please note: The photographed home may have been modified to suit homeowner preferences. If you order plans, have a builder or design professional check them against the photograph to confirm actual construction details.

FIRST FLOOR

- Deck (Optional)
- Raised Hearth
- Family Rm — 15-0 x 17-4
- Brkfst — 9-9 x 14-10
- Kitchen — 12-1 x 13-4
- Ldry
- Garage — 23-8 x 35-4
- Flat Clg @ 9'
- Shelves
- Pantry
- Flat Clg @ 8'
- Parlor — 12-1 x 12-4
- DN
- UP
- Dining — 11-7 x 12-4
- Porch

CRAWLSPACE/SLAB FOUNDATION OPTION

Design 65004

See Order Pages and Index for Info

Units	Single
Price Code	E
Total Finished	2,300 sq. ft.
First Finished	1,067 sq. ft.
Second Finished	1,233 sq. ft.
Basement Unfinished	1,067 sq. ft.
Dimensions	58'x33'
Foundation	Basement
Bedrooms	3
Full Baths	2
Half Baths	1
First Ceiling	9'2"
Second Ceiling	8'2"
Max Ridge Height	24'6"
Roof Framing	Truss
Exterior Walls	2x6

SECOND FLOOR

FIRST FLOOR

Design 97246

See Order Pages and Index for Info

CAD FILES AVAILABLE
For more information call
800-235-5700

Units	Single
Price Code	E
Total Finished	2,311 sq. ft.
Main Finished	2,311 sq. ft.
Bonus Unfinished	425 sq. ft.
Basement Unfinished	2,311 sq. ft.
Garage Unfinished	500 sq. ft.
Dimensions	61'x65'4"
Foundation	Basement Crawlspace
Bedrooms	4
Full Baths	2
Half Baths	1
First Ceiling	9'
Second Ceiling	8'
Max Ridge Height	26'8"
Roof Framing	Stick
Exterior Walls	2x4

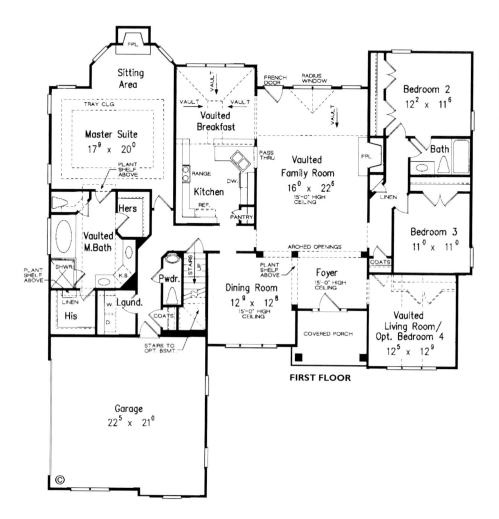

FIRST FLOOR

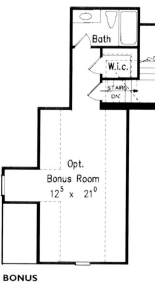

BONUS

Design 97857

See Order Pages and Index for Info

Units	Single
Price Code	E
Total Finished	2,332 sq. ft.
Main Finished	2,332 sq. ft.
Garage Unfinished	620 sq. ft.
Deck Unfinished	80 sq. ft.
Porch Unfinished	48 sq. ft.
Dimensions	82'3"x86'6"
Foundation	Slab
Bedrooms	3
Full Baths	2
Half Baths	1
Main Ceiling	9'-10'
Max Ridge Height	29'
Roof Framing	Stick
Exterior Walls	2x4

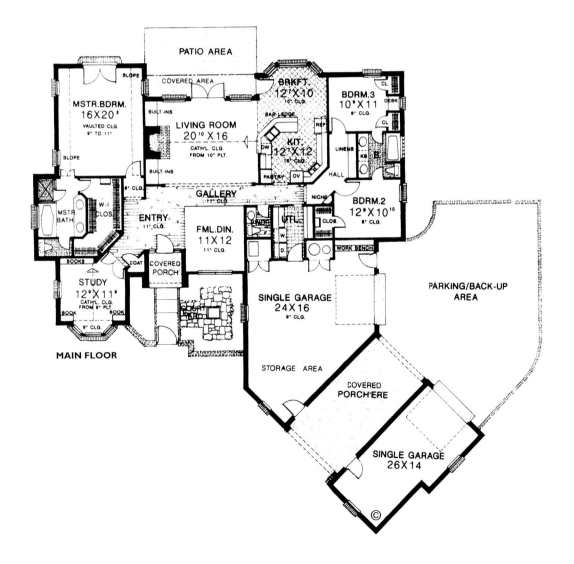

Design 98455

See Order Pages and Index for Info

Units	Single
Price Code	E
Total Finished	2,349 sq. ft.
First Finished	1,761 sq. ft.
Second Finished	588 sq. ft.
Bonus Unfinished	267 sq. ft.
Basement Unfinished	1,761 sq. ft.
Garage Unfinished	435 sq. ft.
Dimensions	56'x47'6"
Foundation	Basement
	Crawlspace
	Slab
Bedrooms	4
Full Baths	3
First Ceiling	9'
Second Ceiling	8'
Max Ridge Height	31'6"
Roof Framing	Stick
Exterior Walls	2x4

CAD **FILES AVAILABLE**
For more information call
800-235-7700

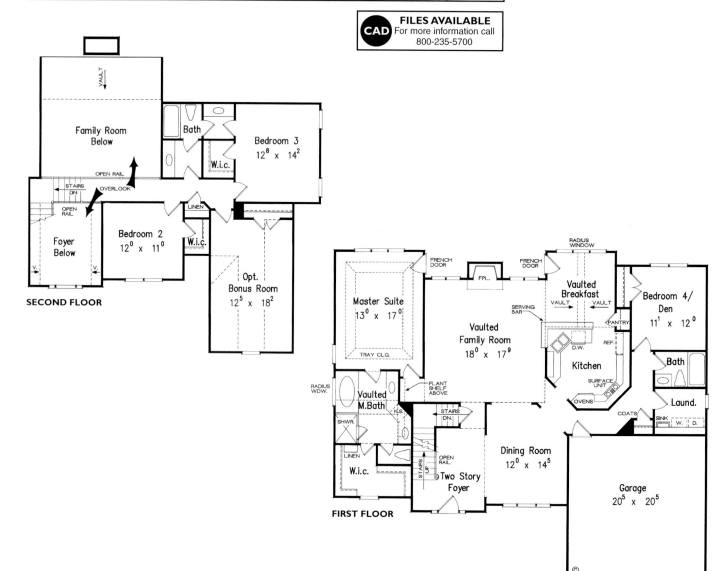

Design **57075**

See Order Pages and Index for Info

Units	Single
Price Code	Please call for pricing
Total Finished	3,129 sq. ft.
First Finished	2,357 sq. ft.
Second Finished	772 sq. ft.
Bonus Unfinished	450 sq. ft.
Dimensions	69'4"x67'4"
Foundation	Crawlspace
Bedrooms	4
Full Baths	2
3/4 Baths	1
Max Ridge Height	30'6"
Roof Framing	Stick
Exterior Walls	2x4

Hot New Design

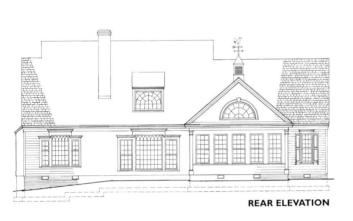

REAR ELEVATION

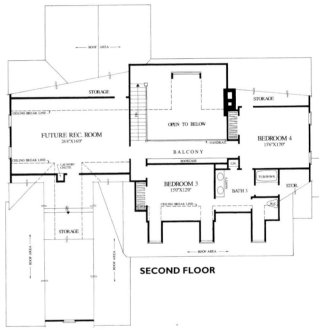

SECOND FLOOR

FIRST FLOOR

Design **57004**

See Order Pages and Index for Info

Units	Single
Price Code	Please call for pricing
Total Finished	2,380 sq. ft.
First Finished	1,712 sq. ft.
Second Finished	668 sq. ft.
Bonus Unfinished	573 sq. ft.
Dimensions	86'x50'2"
Foundation	Combo Basement/ Crawlspace
Bedrooms	3
Full Baths	2
Half Baths	1
First Ceiling	9'
Max Ridge Height	28'
Roof Framing	Stick
Exterior Walls	2x4

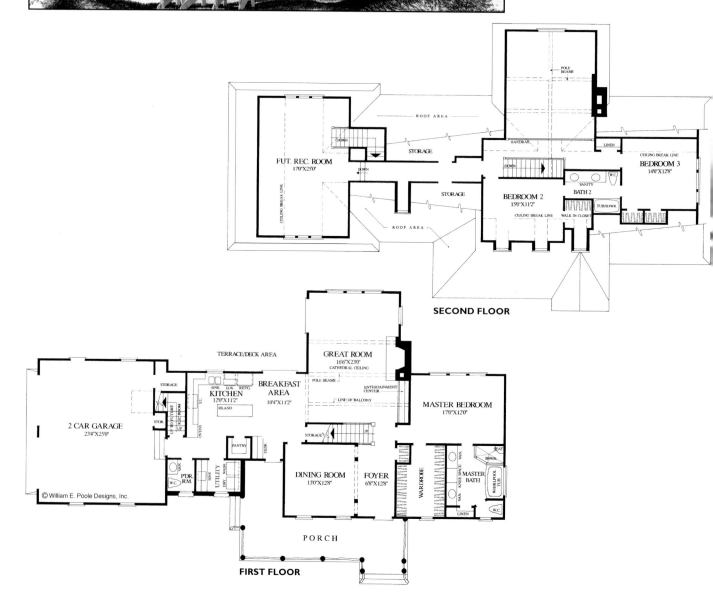

SECOND FLOOR

FIRST FLOOR

© William E. Poole Designs, Inc.

Design 24262

See Order Pages and Index for Info

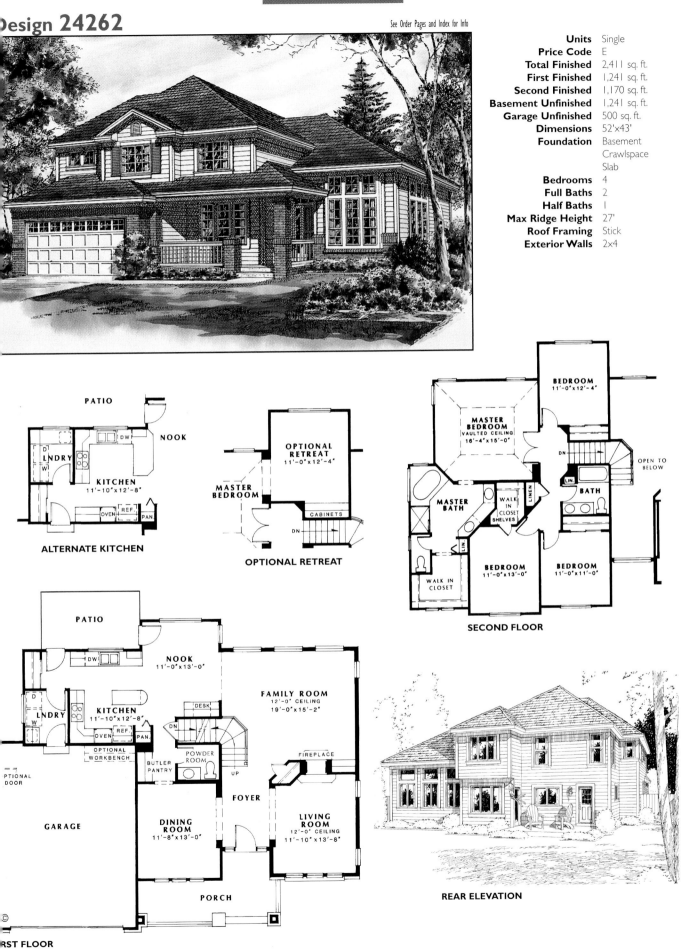

Units	Single
Price Code	E
Total Finished	2,411 sq. ft.
First Finished	1,241 sq. ft.
Second Finished	1,170 sq. ft.
Basement Unfinished	1,241 sq. ft.
Garage Unfinished	500 sq. ft.
Dimensions	52'x43'
Foundation	Basement Crawlspace Slab
Bedrooms	4
Full Baths	2
Half Baths	1
Max Ridge Height	27'
Roof Framing	Stick
Exterior Walls	2x4

PATIO

NOOK

LNDRY

KITCHEN
11'-10"x12'-8"

ALTERNATE KITCHEN

OPTIONAL RETREAT
11'-0"x12'-4"

MASTER BEDROOM

CABINETS

DN

OPTIONAL RETREAT

BEDROOM
11'-0"x12'-4"

MASTER BEDROOM
VAULTED CEILING
16'-4"x15'-0"

DN

OPEN TO BELOW

LINEN

MASTER BATH

WALK IN CLOSET SHELVES

LIN

BATH

LIN

WALK IN CLOSET

BEDROOM
11'-0"x13'-0"

BEDROOM
11'-0"x11'-0"

SECOND FLOOR

PATIO

NOOK
11'-0"x13'-0"

LNDRY

KITCHEN
11'-10"x12'-8"

OVEN REF PAN

OPTIONAL WORKBENCH

BUTLER PANTRY

DESK

DN

POWDER ROOM

UP

FAMILY ROOM
12'-0" CEILING
19'-0"x15'-2"

FIREPLACE

FOYER

GARAGE

OPTIONAL DOOR

DINING ROOM
11'-8"x13'-0"

LIVING ROOM
12'-0" CEILING
11'-10"x13'-8"

PORCH

FIRST FLOOR

REAR ELEVATION

Design 57007

See Order Pages and Index for Info

© William E Poole Designs, Inc.

Units	Single
Price Code	Please call for pricing
Total Finished	2,419 sq. ft.
First Finished	1,776 sq. ft.
Second Finished	643 sq. ft.
Bonus Unfinished	367 sq. ft.
Dimensions	61'8"x74'4"
Foundation	Combo Basement/ Crawlspace
Bedrooms	4
Full Baths	3
Max Ridge Height	29'
Roof Framing	Stick
Exterior Walls	2x4

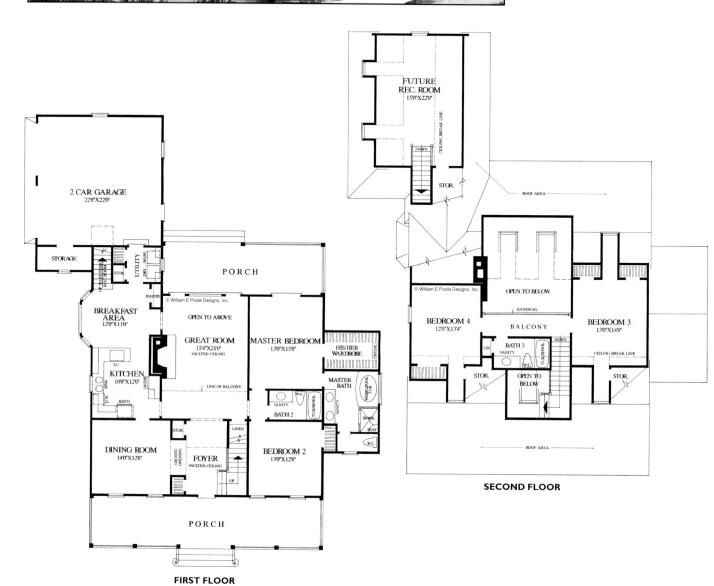

FIRST FLOOR

SECOND FLOOR

Design **57003**

See Order Pages and Index for Info

PHOTOGRAPHY & LINE ART: COURTESY OF WILLIAM E. POOLE ARCHITECTS, INC.

Units	Single
Price Code	Please call for pricing
Total Finished	2,438 sq. ft.
First Finished	1,704 sq. ft.
Second Finished	734 sq. ft.
Bonus Unfinished	479 sq. ft.
Dimensions	50'x82'6"
Foundation	Basement
Bedrooms	3
Full Baths	4
Half Baths	1
Max Ridge Height	33'
Roof Framing	Stick
Exterior Walls	2x4

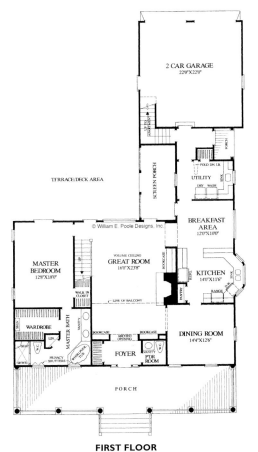

FIRST FLOOR

Please note: The photographed home may have been modified to suit homeowner preferences. If you order plans, have a builder or design professional check them against the photograph to confirm actual construction details.

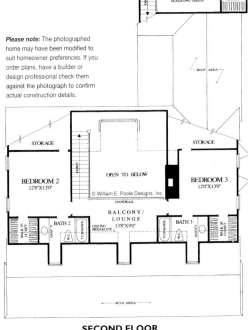

SECOND FLOOR

REAR ELEVATION

Design 57002

See Order Pages and Index for Info

PHOTOGRAPHY & LINE ART: COURTESY OF WILLIAM E. POOLE ARCHITECTS, INC.

Units	Single
Price Code	Please call for pricing
Total Finished	2,457 sq. ft.
First Finished	1,819 sq. ft.
Second Finished	638 sq. ft.
Bonus Unfinished	385 sq. ft.
Dimensions	47'4"×82'8"
Foundation	Combo Basement/ Crawlspace
Bedrooms	3
Full Baths	2
Half Baths	1
Max Ridge Height	27'
Roof Framing	Stick
Exterior Walls	2×4

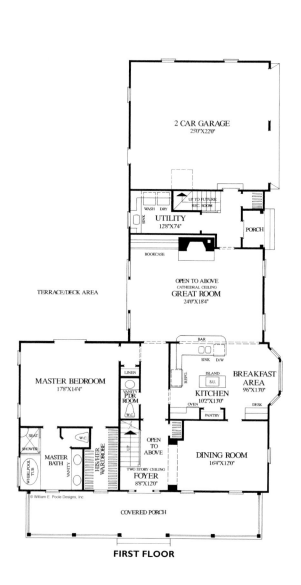

Please note: The photographed home may have been modified to suit homeowner preferences. If you order plans, have a builder or design professional check them against the photograph to confirm actual construction details.

FIRST FLOOR

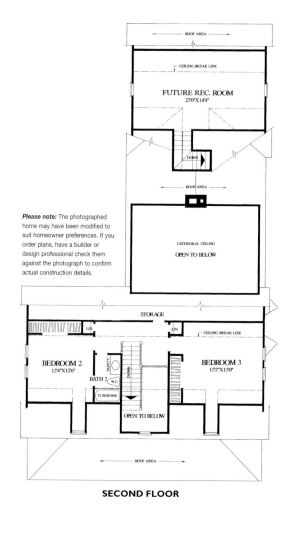

SECOND FLOOR

PHOTOGRAPHY: COURTESY OF THE DESIGNER

above A wide, welcoming porch is crowned by a bold central gable, which has a window that shines onto the two-story foyer.

Please note: The photographed home may have been modified to suit homeowner preferences. If you order plans, you may wish to have a builder or design professional check them against the photographs to confirm construction details.

Design 99431

Price Code	E
Total Finished	2,277 sq. ft.
First Finished	1,570 sq. ft.
Second Finished	707 sq. ft.
Basement Unfinished	1,570 sq. ft.
Garage Unfinished	504 sq. ft.
Dimensions	54'x52'
Foundation	Basement
Bedrooms	4
Full Baths	2
Half Baths	1

hearty WELCOME

From its wide front porch to its spacious country kitchen, this design is inviting to all. The entire first floor of this 2,277-square-foot home is an open plan, so views are clear from the dining room through the great room and into the backyard; or from the kitchen through the breakfast room and great room and out to the side. Separated from the shared spaces is the master suite, which boasts a 9-foot ceiling, ample bath, and large walk-in closet. Upstairs are three secondary bedrooms. This efficient design provides a lot of room at a reasonable price. This home is designed with a basement foundation. Alternate foundations available at an additional charge. Please call 800-235-5700 for more information. 🏛

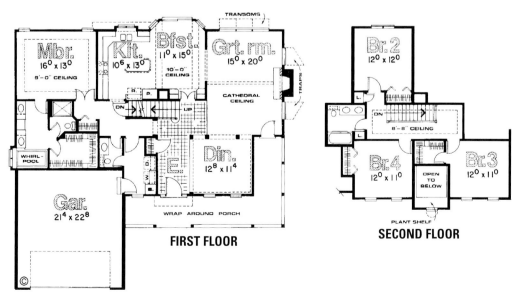

FIRST FLOOR

SECOND FLOOR

classic CRAFTSMAN

above Cedar shingles, a wraparound porch, and a crowning gable outfit this home in traditional Craftsman style.

With its sturdy plank floor and beadboard ceiling, this home's wide front porch is an outdoor sanctuary that provides a place for children to play on a rainy day or for adults to enjoy the outdoors anytime. Built-in cabinets enhance the wide gallery hall that separates the formal and informal living spaces on the 2,018-square-foot first floor. The two-story great-room, with its massive fireplace, dominates the rear of the home. On one end of the great-room, French doors open onto a luminous sunroom. All four bedrooms are on the 1,859-square-foot second floor. The main staircase off the gallery hall rises to the balcony hall that leads to the master suite. A secondary staircase near the kitchen ascends to the wing that houses the three secondary bedrooms and an informal family gathering space. This home is designed with a crawlspace foundation. Please note: This plan is not available for construction in Island, King, Kitsap, Pierce, or Snohomish counties in the state of Washington. ⌂

below A deep wraparound porch with plank flooring and beadboard ceiling easily accommodates a variety of outdoor furnishings.

Order on-line at www.familyhomeplans.com

left The two-story great room features a massive fireplace that both warms and visually dominates the room. At one end of the great room is a sunroom, at the other the kitchen and breakfast area.

below A U-shape kitchen, anchored by a long center island with cooktop, receives light and views from the adjacent sunroom and great room.

Please note: The photographed home may have been modified to suit homeowner preferences. If you order plans, you may wish to have a builder or design professional check them against the photographs to confirm construction details.

Design 32114

Price Code	K
Total Finished	3,877 sq. ft.
First Finished	2,018 sq. ft.
Second Finished	1,859 sq. ft.
Garage Unfinished	816 sq. ft.
Deck Unfinished	867 sq. ft.
Dimensions	86'6"x55'
Foundation	Crawlspace
Bedrooms	4
Full Baths	2
Half Baths	1

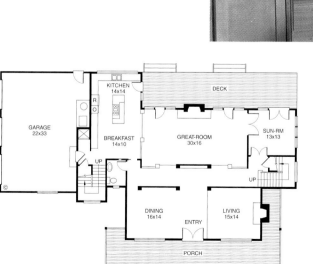

FIRST FLOOR

SECOND FLOOR

PHOTOGRAPHY: MICHAEL PARTENIO

farmhouse FRESH

above A quartet of gables and a covered porch, spanning almost the entire front of the home, form a traditionally elegant design.

Childhood fantasies of the perfect family home take shape with a grown-up attention to detail in this carefully planned farmhouse. Behind a wraparound front porch is 3,767 square feet of living space. In back is a large screen porch the entire family can enjoy in warm weather. The heart of this home is the combined family room, breakfast area, and kitchen.

below The window-filled screen porch brings a bit of the outdoors in, allowing enjoyment of nature in an elegant setting.

The master suite, which is sequestered for privacy, has a tray ceiling, generously sized bath, and two walk-in closets. Included in the master suite is a private study, which also opens onto the balcony that overlooks the entry. Three other bedrooms are on the opposite end of the floor.

A second staircase provides quick access to the kitchen and garage entrance. This home is designed with a basement foundation. 🏛

Order on-line at www.familyhomeplans.com

left While a fireplace casts a cozy glow over the family room, the French doors lining an adjacent wall open it up to the outdoors.

below left The kitchen's design combines plenty of storage space with light decor to keep the work area bright and efficient.

Please note: The photographed home may have been modified to suit homeowner preferences. If you order plans, you may wish to have a builder or design professional check them against the photographs to confirm construction details.

Design 32427

Price Code	K
Total Finished	3,767 sq. ft.
First Finished	1,536 sq. ft.
Second Finished	2,231 sq. ft.
Basement Unfinished	1,536 sq. ft.
Garage Unfinished	704 sq. ft.
Porch Unfinished	476 sq. ft.
Dimensions	72'x44'4"
Foundation	Basement
Bedrooms	4
Full Baths	2
3/4 Baths	1
Half Baths	1

FIRST FLOOR

SECOND FLOOR

a balanced LIFE

above With the garage set back, the home's symmetrical design radiates simple harmony and balance.

Inside, this home's layout speaks to the practical needs of the modern family. A welcoming foyer opens to the formal living and dining rooms, the latter could also be an office for today's work-at-home lifestyle. Past a centralized powder room are the common areas, set into a more open and informal plan. Built-ins and windows define the 1,152-square-foot first floor. On the 940-square-foot second floor, the master suite fills its own wing. A balcony connects the two secondary bedrooms and a full bath with 300 square feet of bonus space that offers possibilities for future expansion. This home is designed with basement, slab, and crawlspace foundation options. 🏛

Design 99696

Price Code	D
Total Finished	2,092 sq. ft.
First Finished	1,152 sq. ft.
Second Finished	940 sq. ft.
Bonus Unfinished	300 sq. ft.
Garage Unfinished	502 sq. ft.
Dimensions	54'x43'
Foundation	Basement Crawlspace Slab
Bedrooms	3
Full Baths	2
Half Baths	1

FIRST FLOOR

INFORMAL DINING 10'-0"x17'-4" 9' CEILING
FR. SL. DR.
LOW WALL
KIT
STORAGE
FAMILY RM 15'-4"x15'-2" 9' CEILING
FP
DESK OR HUTCH 8'-0"x13'-4"
TWO CAR GARAGE 20'-0"x24'-0"
STAIR TO OPT. BSMT
UTIL
PANTRY
FW
LAUN D
LAV
LIVING RM 12'-0"x15'-2" 9' CEILING
DN
UP
FOY
DINING/ OFFICE 12'-0"x13'-0" 9' CEILING
COVERED PORCH

Please note: The photographed home may have been modified to suit homeowner preferences. If you order plans, you may wish to have a builder or design professional check them against the photographs to confirm construction details.

SECOND FLOOR

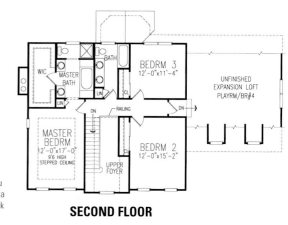

WIC
MASTER BATH
BATH
BEDRM 3 12'-0"x11'-4"
UNFINISHED EXPANSION LOFT PLAYRM/BR#4
LIN
CL
MASTER BEDRM 12'-0"x17'-0" 9'6" HIGH STEPPED CEILING
DN
RAILING
DN
BEDRM 2 12'-0"x15'-2"
UPPER FOYER

Order on-line at www.familyhomeplans.com

PHOTOGRAPHY: HAL LYMAN

above The wraparound porch, culminating in a gazebo (not shown on plan), extends living area outdoors.

so much ROOM

Design 99649

Price Code	H
Total Finished	3,006 sq. ft.
First Finished	1,293 sq. ft.
Second Finished	1,138 sq. ft.
Third Finished	575 sq. ft.
Basement Unfinished	1,293 sq. ft.
Porch Unfinished	585 sq. ft.
Dimensions	63'4"x53'4"
Foundation	Basement
	Slab
Bedrooms	4
Full Baths	3
Half Baths	1

Three floors offer 3,006 square feet of indoor space while, a wraparound porch, and rear terrace allow comfortable outdoor living as well. Inside, each floor is designed for a specific purpose. The first floor is dedicated to the common living areas, yet keeps the formal living and dining rooms separate from the open family room, breakfast area, and kitchen space. The second floor houses all four bedrooms, each with ample closet space and easy access to a full bath. The third floor is reserved for the all-purpose room, which can be as useful as the imagination allows. This home is designed with basement and slab foundation options. 🏛

Please note: The photographed home may have been modified to suit homeowner preferences. If you order plans, you may wish to have a builder or design professional check them against the photographs to confirm construction details.

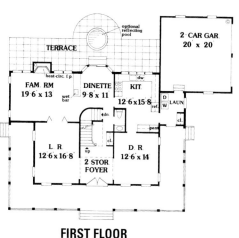

FIRST FLOOR

SECOND FLOOR

THIRD FLOOR

See thousands more plans at www.familyhomeplans.com

151

PHOTOGRAPHY: MICHAEL PARTENIO

victorian COTTAGE

above Doors lead onto the porch from both the kitchen and foyer, emphasizing the spacious Victorian feel and expanding the living space.

below A classic porch off the kitchen offers opportunities for outdoor dining.

Tight city lots are more plentiful than large city lots because they're harder to design for. This light and airy Victorian gives up nothing in style to fit its compact space. Despite the confines of its footprint, the home has a sense of volume and space throughout, even in the entry. The living room, off the foyer, vaults to two stories, with a second-floor loft overhead. Arches and columns take the place of walls to define rooms. Light pours into the interior through oversize windows and glass doors. Skylights add to the radiance. The second-floor master suite has its own private deck. There are 1,090 square feet on the first floor, 701 square feet on the second floor, and 417 square feet on the lower floor. This home is designed with a basement foundation. 🏛

Order on-line at www.familyhomeplans.com

right A raised ceiling adds scale to the detailed family room, which features a fireplace, built-ins, and large windows.

below The unique architectural features of the master bath add artistic appeal to its practicality.

Design 32003

Price Code	D
Total Finished	2,208 sq. ft.
First Finished	1,090 sq. ft.
Second Finished	701 sq. ft.
Lower Finished	417 sq. ft.
Garage Unfinished	552 sq. ft.
Dimensions	34'x42'
Foundation	Basement
Bedrooms	3
Full Baths	3

Please note: The photographed home may have been modified to suit homeowner preferences. If you order plans, you may wish to have a builder or design professional check them against the photographs to confirm construction details.

LOWER FLOOR

FIRST FLOOR

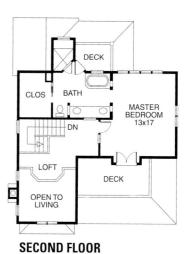

SECOND FLOOR

See thousands more plans at www.familyhomeplans.com

PHOTOGRAPHY: COURTESY OF THE DESIGNER

american TRADITION

above This traditional design offers a comfortable country lifestyle and lots of outdoor space.

below The built-in gazebo brings out the Georgian flavor of this home's architecture.

Melding a pleasing variety of traditional American styles can sometimes result in an overly busy, unfocused design. Here, the mix of Georgian and colonial result in both a satisfying and a highly functional home that builds nicely on its historical country roots.

Mixed with ample private areas are large shared spaces, among them a big family room with hearth and coffered ceiling, a living room that opens to the two-story foyer and dining room beyond, and an efficient kitchen plan that includes a sunny breakfast room. Upstairs is a 340-square-foot playroom for the kids.

The 2,372-square-foot second floor is dominated by the master suite with tray ceiling, a huge master bath with vaulted ceiling, a secluded porch, and private sitting room that overlooks the backyard. Three secondary bedrooms, one with a private bath and the others with a cleverly designed shared bath, round out the second floor.

This home is designed with basement and crawlspace foundation options. 🏛

left The master suite includes a spacious bedroom with adjoining sitting room and see-through fireplace.

below With its recessed sideboard niche, wainscoting, arched entry, and deep crown molding, the formal dining room is an interesting counterpoint to the home's informal areas .

Design 60137

Price Code	L
Total Finished	4,464 sq. ft.
First Finished	2,092 sq. ft.
Second Finished	2,372 sq. ft.
Basement Unfinished	2,092 sq. ft.
Garage Unfinished	674 sq. ft.
Dimensions	75'5"x64'
Foundation	Basement
	Crawlspace
Bedrooms	5
Full Baths	4
Half Baths	1

Please note: The photographed home may have been modified to suit homeowner preferences. If you order plans, you may wish to have a builder or design professional check them against the photographs to confirm construction details.

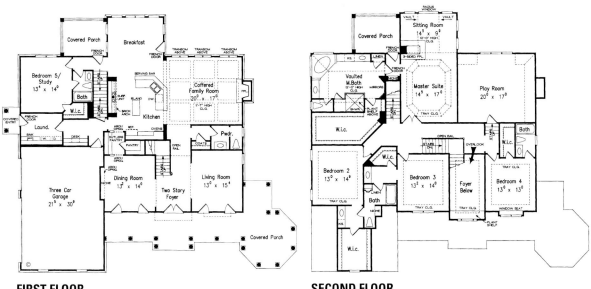

FIRST FLOOR

SECOND FLOOR

above Crisp, clean lines give this home classic appeal, while a centralized arched window and turret-topped gazebo add architectural interest.

design your HOME

This plan allows you to design the home of your dreams by letting you choose how many bedrooms you want. The three-bedroom option opens up the space for a vaulted ceiling in the family room. Promoting casual interaction, the family room opens into the tiled kitchen and breakfast nook. The formal dining area sits on the other side of the kitchen and blends into the living room. A utility area, including garage, completes the plan. This home is designed with a basement foundation. 🏛

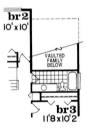

3-BEDROOM OPTION

Design 55024

Price Code	E
Total Finished	2,301 sq. ft.
First Finished	1,180 sq. ft.
Second Finished	1,121 sq. ft.
Garage Unfinished	435 sq. ft.
Dimensions	48'x52'6"
Foundation	Basement
Bedrooms	4
Full Baths	2
Half Baths	1

Please note: The photographed home may have been modified to suit homeowner preferences. If you order plans, you may wish to have a builder or design professional check them against the photographs to confirm construction details.

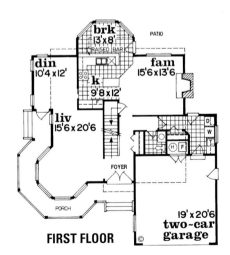

FIRST FLOOR

SECOND FLOOR

PHOTOGRAPHY: JOHN EHRENCLOU

above While this home incorporates a traditional farmhouse design, fine detailing inside and out adds a touch of elegance.

gracious FARMHOUSE

Design 93209

Price Code	E
Total Finished	2,464 sq. ft.
First Finished	1,250 sq. ft.
Second Finished	1,166 sq. ft.
Lower Finished	48 sq. ft.
Basement Unfinished	448 sq. ft.
Garage Unfinished	706 sq. ft.
Dimensions	42'x50'
Foundation	Basement
Bedrooms	4
Full Baths	2
Half Baths	1

Please note: The photographed home may have been modified to suit homeowner preferences. If you order plans, you may wish to have a builder or design professional check them against the photographs to confirm construction details.

Surrounded by porches, this home offers comfortable living inside and out. The open foyer leads directly into the living and dining rooms, and straight ahead into the more informal areas. Here, with only columns to separate it from the breakfast area and kitchen, the great room is an ideal hub for family activity. The second floor is reserved for the bedrooms, including a fabulous master suite with its own private deck. This home is designed with a basement foundation. 🏛

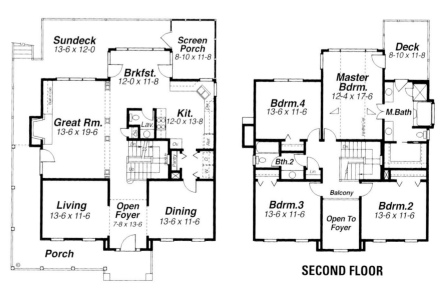

Sundeck 13-6 x 12-0

Screen Porch 8-10 x 11-8

Brkfst. 12-0 x 11-8

Kit. 12-0 x 13-8

Great Rm. 13-6 x 19-6

Lav.

Living 13-6 x 11-6

Open Foyer 7-8 x 13-6

Dining 13-6 x 11-6

Porch

FIRST FLOOR

Deck 8-10 x 11-8

Master Bdrm. 12-4 x 17-6

M.Bath

Bdrm.4 13-6 x 11-6

Bth.2

Lin.

Balcony

Bdrm.3 13-6 x 11-6

Open To Foyer

Bdrm.2 13-6 x 11-6

SECOND FLOOR

everything in its PLACE

above The traditional lines of this home, forming gables and arches, are accented by a striking white trim.

The design of this home offers specific spaces for specific activities. The right wing of the 1,515-square-foot first floor is dedicated to more formal occasions with its living and dining rooms. French doors and high ceilings contribute to the elegance of each room. In the rear, the kitchen is designed with plenty of work space, keeping both the gourmet chef and the weekend cook in mind. The vaulted family room offers space for more casual gatherings and is open to the breakfast/kitchen area. On the 1,203-square-foot second floor, the master suite occupies the right wing. A balcony, overlooking the foyer and family room, connects the suite to the secondary bedrooms, a full bath, and the loft, which can also serve as a fourth bedroom. The plan also offers an optional closet in the loft. This home is designed with basement, slab, and crawlspace foundation options. 🏛

below Aside from aesthetic purposes, the kitchen's island, with its prep sink and serving space, offers a world of efficiency.

above A wall of windows keeps the breakfast room bright and cheery, spilling its light into the efficient kitchen.

left A hardwood floor, French doors, and classic trim molding topped by a 9-foot ceiling creates formal charm in the dining room.

Design 99693

Price Code	F
Total Finished	2,178 sq. ft.
First Finished	1,515 sq. ft.
Second Finished	1,203 sq. ft.
Garage Unfinished	475 sq. ft.
Porch Unfinished	266 sq. ft.
Dimensions	56'x45'
Foundation	Basement
	Crawlspace
	Slab
Bedrooms	4
Full Baths	2
Half Baths	1

Please note: The photographed home may have been modified to suit homeowner preferences. If you order plans, you may wish to have a builder or design professional check them against the photographs to confirm construction details.

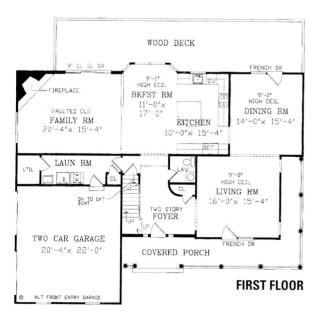

FIRST FLOOR

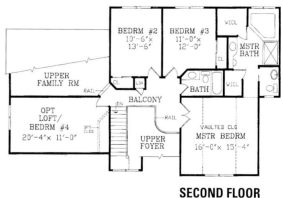

SECOND FLOOR

PHOTOGRAPHY: COURTESY OF THE DESIGNER

practical COUNTRY

above A quartet of gables, a bay window, and a covered porch lend a welcoming face to this classic.

To the left, inside the tiled entry is the dining room with its built-in hutch and curio cabinet. The large kitchen opens to the window-lined breakfast nook and features ample counter space, including a central island; a built-in desk adds to the efficiency. The family room and formal living room, directly across from the dining room, round out the 1,093-square-foot first floor. All four bedrooms fill the 1,038-square-foot second floor. This home is designed with a basement foundation. Alternate foundation options are available at an additional charge. Please call 800-235-5700 for additional information. 🏛

Design 94941

Price Code	D
Total Finished	2,131 sq. ft.
First Finished	1,093 sq. ft.
Second Finished	1,038 sq. ft.
Basement Unfinished	1,093 sq. ft.
Garage Unfinished	527 sq. ft.
Dimensions	55'4"x37'8"
Foundation	Basement
Bedrooms	4
Full Baths	2
Half Baths	1

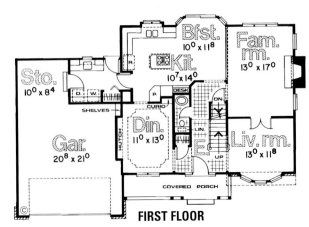

FIRST FLOOR

SECOND FLOOR

Please note: The photographed home may have been modified to suit homeowner preferences. If you order plans, you may wish to have a builder or design professional check them against the photographs to confirm construction details.

Design 24653

See Order Pages and Index for Info

PHOTOGRAPHY: COURTESY OF THE DESIGNER

Units	Single
Price Code	F
Total Finished	2,578 sq. ft.
First Finished	1,245 sq. ft.
Second Finished	1,333 sq. ft.
Bonus Unfinished	192 sq. ft.
Basement Unfinished	1,245 sq. ft.
Garage Unfinished	614 sq. ft.
Dimensions	50'x46'
Foundation	Basement
	Crawlspace
	Slab
Bedrooms	3
Full Baths	2
Half Baths	1
First Ceiling	9'
Second Ceiling	8'
Max Ridge Height	35'
Roof Framing	Stick
Exterior Walls	2x4

ase note: The photographed
me may have been modified to
homeowner preferences. If you
er plans, have a builder or
sign professional check them
inst the photograph to confirm
ual construction details.

**CRAWLSPACE/SLAB
FOUNDATION OPTION**

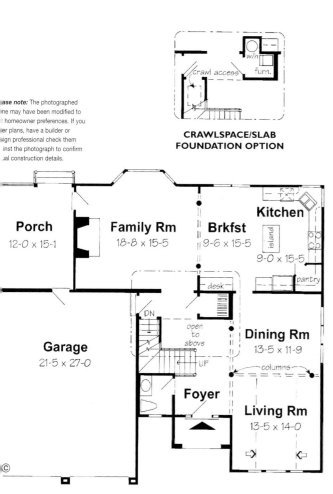

RST FLOOR

SECOND FLOOR

Design 98426

See Order Pages and Index for Info

Units	Single
Price Code	F
Total Finished	2,622 sq. ft.
Main Finished	2,622 sq. ft.
Bonus Unfinished	478 sq. ft.
Basement Unfinished	2,622 sq. ft.
Garage Unfinished	506 sq. ft.
Dimensions	69'x71'4"
Foundation	Basement Crawlspace
Bedrooms	3
Full Baths	2
Half Baths	1
Main Ceiling	9'
Max Ridge Height	29'4"
Roof Framing	Stick
Exterior Walls	2x4

CAD FILES AVAILABLE
For more information call
800-235-5700

Opt. Bonus Room
12⁵ x 23³

BONUS

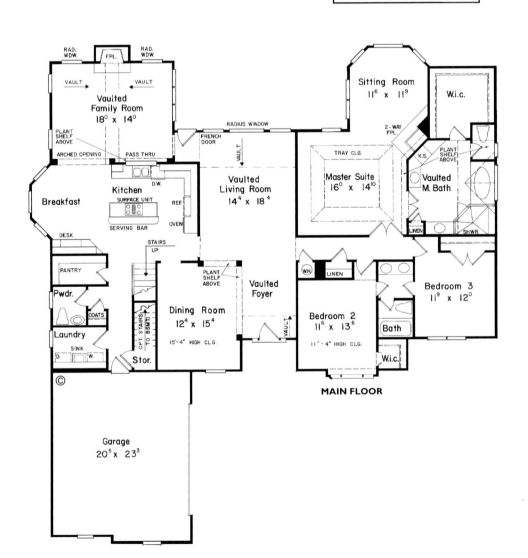

MAIN FLOOR

Design **57056**

See Order Pages and Index for Info

Units	Single
Price Code	Please call for pricing
Total Finished	2,630 sq. ft.
First Finished	1,970 sq. ft.
Second Finished	660 sq. ft.
Bonus Unfinished	424 sq. ft.
Dimensions	62'6"x79'10"
Foundation	Basement
Bedrooms	3
Full Baths	2
Half Baths	1
Max Ridge Height	28'
Roof Framing	Stick
Exterior Walls	2x4

Hot New Design

FUTURE REC. ROOM
15'0"X24'0"

STORAGE

2 CAR GARAGE
22'0"X24'0"

STORAGE

ROOF AREA

STORAGE

UTILITY

REAR ENTRY

BEDROOM 2
13'6"X12'4"

OPEN TO BELOW

BALCONY

BEDROOM 3
17'4"X12'0"

CEILING BREAK LINE

HANDRAIL

WALK IN CLOSET

BATH 2
VANITY

STORAGE

ROOF AREA

TERRACE/DECK AREA

PORCH

PDR. ROOM
VANITY
W.C.

SECOND FLOOR

MASTER BEDROOM
13'6"X17'4"

GREAT ROOM
VAULTED CEILING
21'4"X17'4"

KITCHEN
14'10"X13'0"

LINE OF BALCONY

BOOKCASE

DESK

OVENS

REFR.

SINK

D/W

BAR
ISLAND

© William E. Poole Designs, Inc.

PANTRY

SHOWER

SEAT

MASTER BATH

VANITY

PRIVACY SHUTTERS

HIS/HER WARDROBE

LINEN

FOYER
7'0"X13'0"

DINING ROOM
15'0"X13'0"

CHINA/SILVER

BREAKFAST AREA
12'10"X11'0"

PORCH

FIRST FLOOR

REAR ELEVATION

Design 24403

See Order Pages and Index for Info

PHOTOGRAPHY: COURTESY OF THE DESIGNER

Units	Single
Price Code	F
Total Finished	2,647 sq. ft.
First Finished	1,378 sq. ft.
Second Finished	1,269 sq. ft.
Basement Unfinished	1,378 sq. ft.
Garage Unfinished	717 sq. ft.
Dimensions	71'x45'
Foundation	Basement
	Crawlspace
	Slab
Bedrooms	4
Full Baths	2
3/4 Baths	1
First Ceiling	9'
Second Ceiling	8'
Max Ridge Height	29'
Roof Framing	Stick
Exterior Walls	2x4

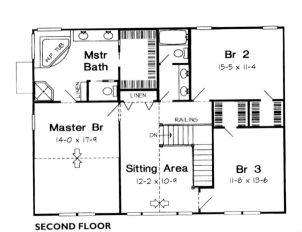

SECOND FLOOR

REAR ELEVATION

Please note: The photographed home may have been modified to suit homeowner preferences. If you order plans, have a builder or design professional check them against the photograph to confirm actual construction details.

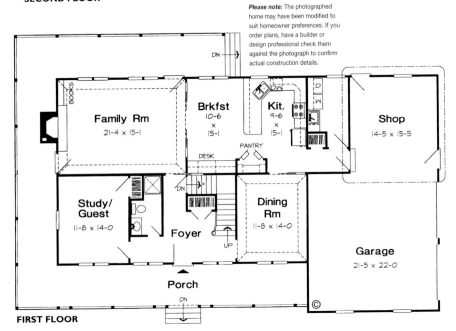

FIRST FLOOR

**CRAWLSPACE/SLAB
FOUNDATION OPTION**

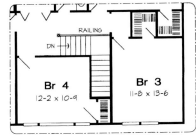

OPTIONAL SECOND FLOOR

esign **97946**

See Order Pages and Index for Info

SECOND FLOOR

- PLAY ROOM 16' X 16'
- WINDOW SEAT
- SLOPE
- ATTIC
- AC
- DN
- BEDROOM 2 11'6" X 13'6"
- BEDROOM 3 10'8" X 15'
- BEDROOM 4 12'6" X 11'4"
- LIN
- SLOPE

Units	Single
Price Code	F
Total Finished	2,688 sq. ft.
First Finished	1,650 sq. ft.
Second Finished	1,038 sq. ft.
Garage Unfinished	601 sq. ft.
Deck Unfinished	226 sq. ft.
Dimensions	50'x60'
Foundation	Basement
Bedrooms	4
Full Baths	3
Half Baths	1
First Ceiling	9'
Second Ceiling	8'
Max Ridge Height	30'
Roof Framing	Stick
Exterior Walls	2x4

* Alternate foundation options available at an additional charge.
Please call 1-800-235-5700 for more information.

FIRST FLOOR

- NOOK 12'4" X 11'8"
- EATING BAR
- KITCHEN 13" X 12'
- ISLAND
- PANTRY
- UP
- LIVING ROOM 16' X 19'6" 9' CLG.
- OPTIONAL BASEMENT STAIRS
- MASTER SUITE 16'2" X 13'6" 11' CLG.
- AC
- 9' CLG.
- DINING ROOM 10'8" X 15'
- FOYER 9' CLG
- OPTIONAL STUDY
- 3 CAR GARAGE 20'4" X 28'6"
- PORCH
- D W

esign **62006**

See Order Pages and Index for Info

GREAT ROOM

PHOTOGRAPHY: COURTESY OF THE DESIGNER

Please note: The photographed home may have been modified to suit homeowner preferences. If you order plans, have a builder or design professional check them against the photograph to confirm actual construction details.

Units	Single
Price Code	F
Total Finished	2,701 sq. ft.
First Finished	2,352 sq. ft.
Second Finished	349 sq. ft.
Garage Unfinished	697 sq. ft.
Porch Unfinished	724 sq. ft.
Dimensions	69'x69'10"
Foundation	Basement
	Crawlspace
	Slab
Bedrooms	3
Full Baths	2
3/4 Baths	2
Half Baths	1
First Ceiling	9'
Second Ceiling	8'
Roof Framing	Stick
Exterior Walls	2x4

SECOND FLOOR

- VAULT
- OPEN TO BELOW
- 8' LINE
- GAME ROOM 22'-2" X 14'-6"
- DN
- 8' WALL

FIRST FLOOR

- GLASS BLOCKS
- WHP TUB
- M. BATH 19'-4" X 11'-4"
- PLANTER
- 10' BOX COL
- PLANTER
- ATRIUM DOOR
- MASTER SUITE 19'-4" X 13'-8"
- 10' PORCH
- DESK
- ATRIUM DOOR
- MEDIA CENTER
- BREAKFAST ROOM 12'-2" X 8'-4"
- OPEN ABOVE
- DW
- BEDROOM 3 16'-9" X 12'-2"
- GREAT ROOM 20'-2" X 20'-6"
- ISLAND
- OVEN
- LAU. 9'-10" X 10'-6"
- STOR.
- KNEE SPACE
- LIN
- UP
- KITCHEN 12'-2" X 16'-2"
- REF
- BATH
- NICHE
- PAN
- 8' COLUMN
- BEDROOM 2 13'-2" X 14'-8"
- BATH
- WINDOW SEAT
- FOYER 18' CEILING
- DINING 9' CEILING 12'-4" X 12'-8"
- DESK
- GARAGE 21'-4" X 32'-8"
- PORCH 31'-0" X 8'-0"
- 18' COLUMNS

Design 98528

See Order Pages and Index for Info

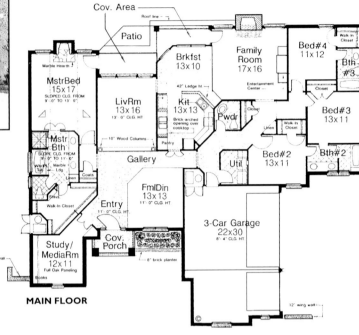

MAIN FLOOR

Units	Single
Price Code	F
Total Finished	2,748 sq. ft.
Main Finished	2,748 sq. ft.
Garage Unfinished	660 sq. ft.
Deck Unfinished	212 sq. ft.
Porch Unfinished	72 sq. ft.
Dimensions	75'x64'5"
Foundation	Slab
Bedrooms	4
Full Baths	3
Half Baths	I
Max Ridge Height	31'6"
Roof Framing	Stick
Exterior Walls	2x4

Design 90443

See Order Pages and Index for Info

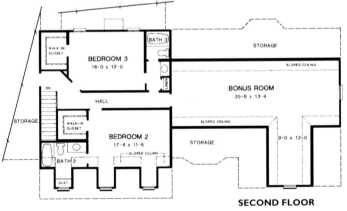

SECOND FLOOR

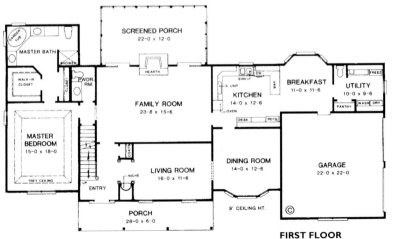

FIRST FLOOR

Units	Single
Price Code	G
Total Finished	2,759 sq. ft.
First Finished	1,927 sq. ft.
Second Finished	832 sq. ft.
Bonus Unfinished	624 sq. ft.
Basement Unfinished	1,674 sq. ft.
Dimensions	79'4"x46'
Foundation	Basement
	Crawlspace
	Slab
Bedrooms	3
Full Baths	3
Half Baths	2
First Ceiling	9'
Max Ridge Height	28'
Roof Framing	Stick
Exterior Walls	2x4

Design 98494

See Order Pages and Index for Info

Units	Single
Price Code	G
Total Finished	2,772 sq. ft.
First Finished	1,447 sq. ft.
Second Finished	1,325 sq. ft.
Bonus Unfinished	301 sq. ft.
Basement Unfinished	1,447 sq. ft.
Garage Unfinished	393 sq. ft.
Dimensions	56'4"x41'
Foundation	Basement Crawlspace
Bedrooms	5
Full Baths	4
First Ceiling	9'
Second Ceiling	8'
Max Ridge Height	32'
Roof Framing	Stick
Exterior Walls	2x4

CAD FILES AVAILABLE
For more information call
800-235-5700

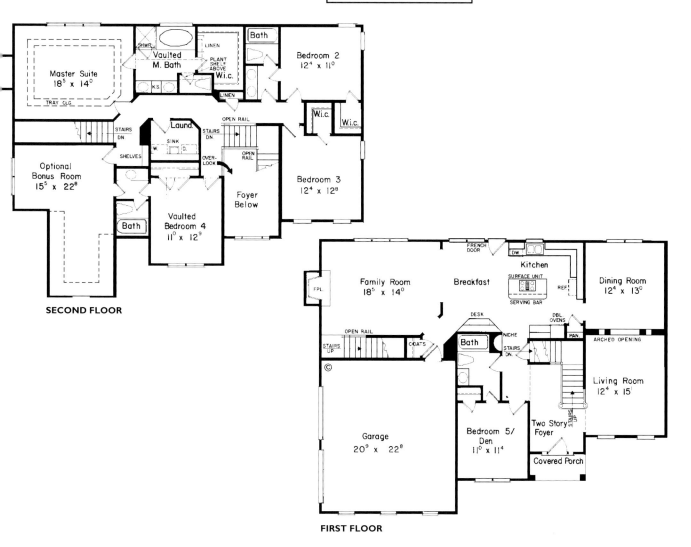

SECOND FLOOR

Master Suite 18⁵ x 14⁰
Vaulted M. Bath
Bath
Bedroom 2 12⁴ x 11⁰
Optional Bonus Room 15⁵ x 22⁸
Laund.
Foyer Below
Bedroom 3 12⁴ x 12⁸
Bath
Vaulted Bedroom 4 11⁰ x 12⁹

FIRST FLOOR

Family Room 18⁵ x 14⁰
Breakfast
Kitchen
Dining Room 12⁴ x 13⁰
Living Room 12⁴ x 15¹
Garage 20⁹ x 22⁸
Bath
Bedroom 5/ Den 11⁰ x 11⁴
Two Story Foyer
Covered Porch

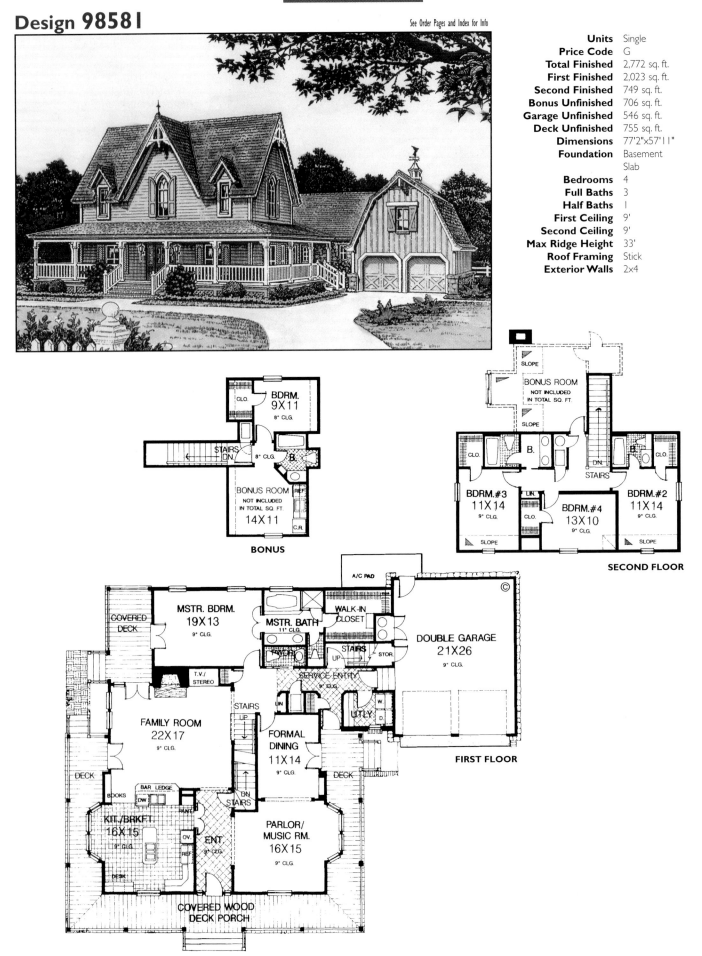

1-800-235-5700 or www.familyhomeplans.com

Design 98581

See Order Pages and Index for Info

Units	Single
Price Code	G
Total Finished	2,772 sq. ft.
First Finished	2,023 sq. ft.
Second Finished	749 sq. ft.
Bonus Unfinished	706 sq. ft.
Garage Unfinished	546 sq. ft.
Deck Unfinished	755 sq. ft.
Dimensions	77'2"x57'11"
Foundation	Basement Slab
Bedrooms	4
Full Baths	3
Half Baths	1
First Ceiling	9'
Second Ceiling	9'
Max Ridge Height	33'
Roof Framing	Stick
Exterior Walls	2x4

BONUS

SECOND FLOOR

FIRST FLOOR

Design 57076

See Order Pages and Index for Info

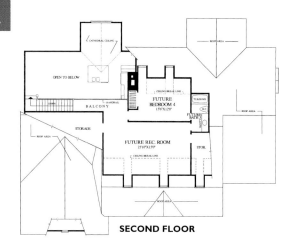

SECOND FLOOR

Units	Single
Price Code	Please call for pricing
Total Finished	2,777 sq. ft.
Main Finished	2,777 sq. ft.
Bonus Unfinished	733 sq. ft.
Basement Unfinished	2,777 sq. ft.
Dimensions	75'6"x60'2"
Foundation	Crawlspace
Bedrooms	3
Full Baths	2
Half Baths	1
Max Ridge Height	29'6"
Roof Framing	Stick
Exterior Walls	2x4

Hot New Design

FIRST FLOOR

REAR ELEVATION

Design 98536

See Order Pages and Index for Info

BONUS

Units	Single
Price Code	1
Total Finished	2,787 sq. ft.
Main Finished	2,787 sq. ft.
Bonus Unfinished	636 sq. ft.
Garage Unfinished	832 sq. ft.
Deck Unfinished	152 sq. ft.
Porch Unfinished	212 sq. ft.
Dimensions	101'x58'8"
Foundation	Crawlspace / Slab
Bedrooms	4
Full Baths	2
Half Baths	1
Main Ceiling	9'
Second Ceiling	7'-9'
Max Ridge Height	28'6"
Roof Framing	Stick
Exterior Walls	2x4

MAIN FLOOR

Design 32400

See Order Pages and Index for Info

PHOTOGRAPHY: JON MILLER, HEDRICH-BLESSING

Units	Single
Price Code	G
Total Finished	2,823 sq. ft.
First Finished	1,893 sq. ft.
Second Finished	930 sq. ft.
Bonus Unfinished	386 sq. ft.
Basement Unfinished	1,692 sq. ft.
Garage Unfinished	926 sq. ft.
Dimensions	62'8"x81'
Foundation	Basement
Bedrooms	3
Full Baths	3
First Ceiling	9'
Second Ceiling	8'
Vaulted Ceiling	17'
Max Ridge Height	31'4"
Roof Framing	Truss
Exterior Walls	2x4

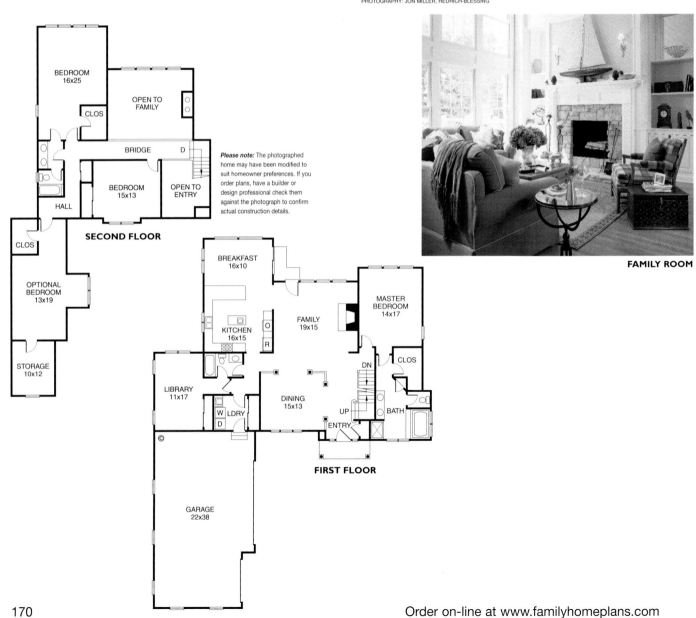

FAMILY ROOM

Please note: The photographed home may have been modified to suit homeowner preferences. If you order plans, have a builder or design professional check them against the photograph to confirm actual construction details.

SECOND FLOOR

FIRST FLOOR

Design 57059

See Order Pages and Index for Info

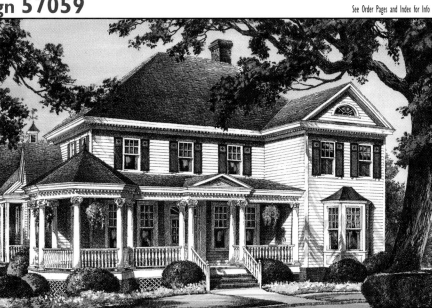

Units	Single
Price Code	Please call for pricing
Total Finished	2,825 sq. ft.
First Finished	1,734 sq. ft.
Second Finished	1,091 sq. ft.
Bonus Unfinished	488 sq. ft.
Dimensions	57'6"×80'11"
Foundation	Basement Crawlspace
Bedrooms	4
Full Baths	3
Half Baths	1
First Ceiling	10'
Max Ridge Height	6'8"
Roof Framing	Stick
Exterior Walls	2x4

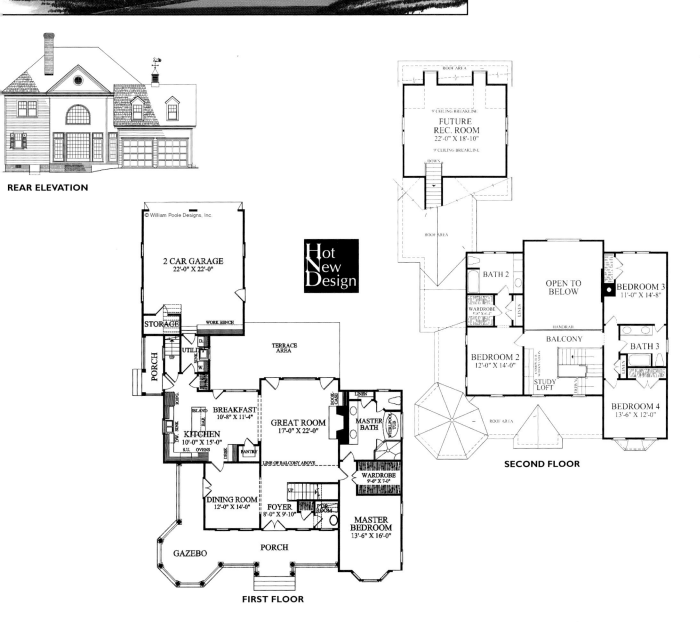

REAR ELEVATION

FUTURE REC. ROOM
22'-0" X 18'-10"

SECOND FLOOR

BEDROOM 3
11'-0" X 14'-8"

BATH 3

BEDROOM 4
13'-6" X 12'-0"

OPEN TO BELOW

BATH 2

WARDROBE

BALCONY

BEDROOM 2
12'-0" X 14'-0"

STUDY LOFT

© William Poole Designs, Inc.

2 CAR GARAGE
22'-0" X 22'-0"

Hot New Design

STORAGE

WORK BENCH

UTILITY

TERRACE AREA

BREAKFAST
10'-8" X 11'-4"

KITCHEN
10'-0" X 15'-0"

GREAT ROOM
17'-0" X 22'-0"

MASTER BATH

LINEN

DINING ROOM
12'-0" X 14'-0"

FOYER
8'-0" X 9'-10"

PDR ROOM

WARDROBE
9'-6" X 7-0"

MASTER BEDROOM
13'-6" X 16'-0"

GAZEBO

PORCH

FIRST FLOOR

Design 92576

See Order Pages and Index for Info

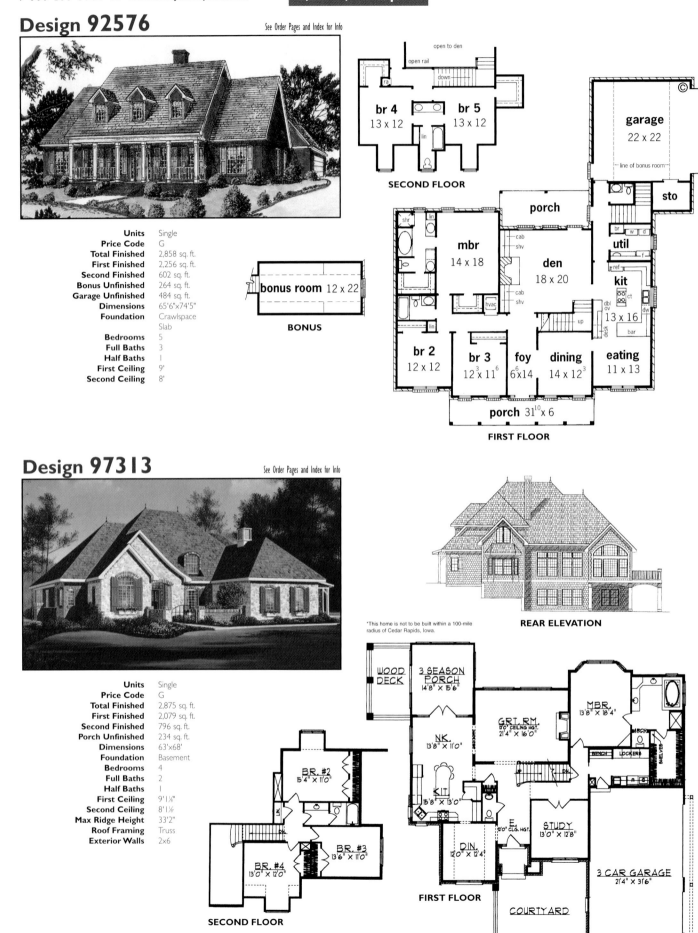

Units	Single
Price Code	G
Total Finished	2,858 sq. ft.
First Finished	2,256 sq. ft.
Second Finished	602 sq. ft.
Bonus Unfinished	264 sq. ft.
Garage Unfinished	484 sq. ft.
Dimensions	65'6"x74'5"
Foundation	Crawlspace
	Slab
Bedrooms	5
Full Baths	3
Half Baths	1
First Ceiling	9'
Second Ceiling	8'

SECOND FLOOR

bonus room 12 x 22

BONUS

FIRST FLOOR

Design 97313

See Order Pages and Index for Info

REAR ELEVATION

*This home is not to be built within a 100-mile radius of Cedar Rapids, Iowa.

Units	Single
Price Code	G
Total Finished	2,875 sq. ft.
First Finished	2,079 sq. ft.
Second Finished	796 sq. ft.
Porch Unfinished	234 sq. ft.
Dimensions	63'x68'
Foundation	Basement
Bedrooms	4
Full Baths	2
Half Baths	1
First Ceiling	9'1⅛"
Second Ceiling	8'1⅛"
Max Ridge Height	33'2"
Roof Framing	Truss
Exterior Walls	2x6

SECOND FLOOR

FIRST FLOOR

esign 97220

See Order Pages and Index for Info

Units	Single
Price Code	G
Total Finished	2,892 sq. ft.
First Finished	1,269 sq. ft.
Second Finished	1,623 sq. ft.
Basement Unfinished	1,269 sq. ft.
Garage Unfinished	672 sq. ft.
Dimensions	58'x41'6"
Foundation	Basement
	Crawlspace
Bedrooms	4
Full Baths	3
Half Baths	1
Max Ridge Height	33'
Roof Framing	Stick
Exterior Walls	2x4

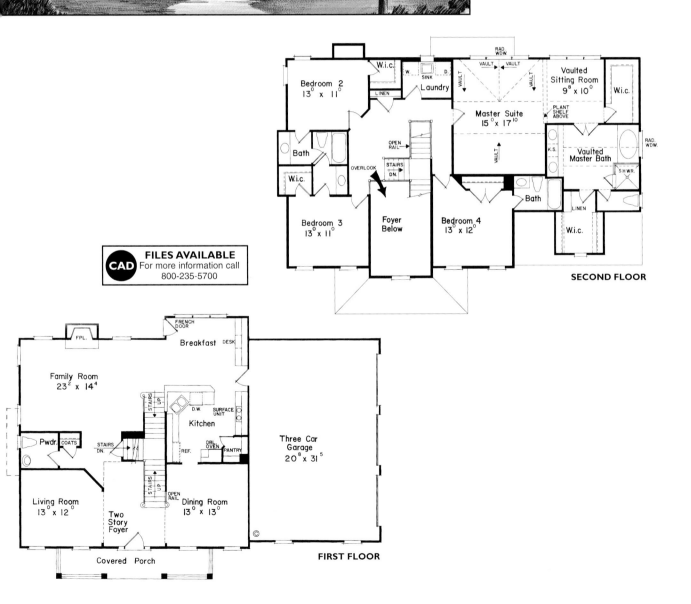

FILES AVAILABLE
CAD For more information call
800-235-5700

SECOND FLOOR

FIRST FLOOR

Design 98458

See Order Pages and Index for Info

Units	Single
Price Code	G
Total Finished	2,940 sq. ft.
First Finished	2,044 sq. ft.
Second Finished	896 sq. ft.
Bonus Unfinished	197 sq. ft.
Basement Unfinished	2,044 sq. ft.
Garage Unfinished	544 sq. ft.
Dimensions	63'x54'
Foundation	Basement
	Crawlspace
	Slab
Bedrooms	4
Full Baths	3
Half Baths	1
First Ceiling	9'
Second Ceiling	8'
Max Ridge Height	31'4"
Roof Framing	Stick
Exterior Walls	2x4

CAD FILES AVAILABLE
For more information call
800-235-7700

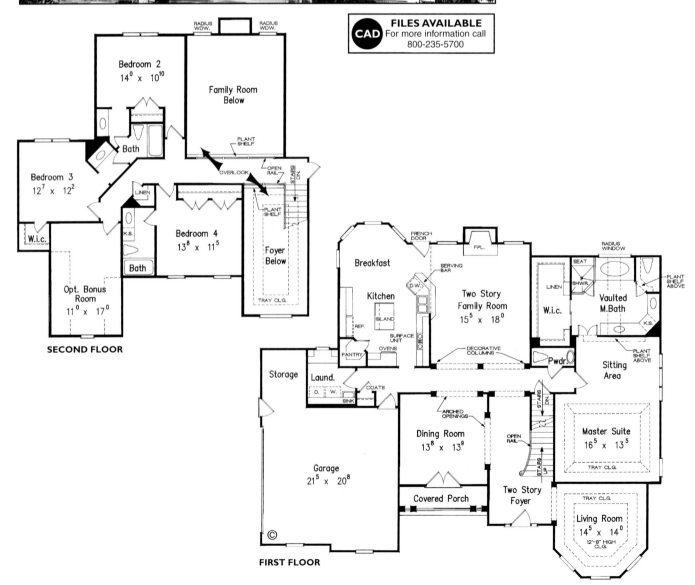

SECOND FLOOR

FIRST FLOOR

Design 98534

See Order Pages and Index for Info

Units	Single
Price Code	G
Total Finished	2,959 sq. ft.
First Finished	1,848 sq. ft.
Second Finished	1,111 sq. ft.
Garage Unfinished	722 sq. ft.
Deck Unfinished	172 sq. ft.
Porch Unfinished	42 sq. ft.
Dimensions	73'4"x44'
Foundation	Crawlspace
	Slab
Bedrooms	4
Full Baths	2
3/4 Baths	1
Half Baths	1
First Ceiling	9'
Second Ceiling	8'
Max Ridge Height	32'
Roof Framing	Stick
Exterior Walls	2x4

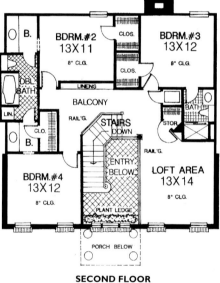

SECOND FLOOR

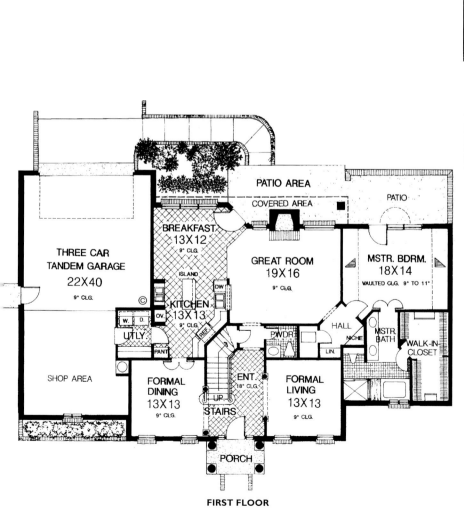

FIRST FLOOR

Design 32353

See Order Pages and Index for Info

PHOTOGRAPHY: LAURIE BLACK

Units	Single
Price Code	G
Total Finished	2,977 sq. ft.
First Finished	2,111 sq. ft.
Second Finished	866 sq. ft.
Garage Unfinished	912 sq. ft.
Deck Unfinished	948 sq. ft.
Dimensions	76'x93'
Foundation	Crawlspace
Bedrooms	3
Full Baths	1
3/4 Baths	1
Half Baths	1
First Ceiling	8'
Second Ceiling	8'
Vaulted Ceiling	23'2"
Max Ridge Height	29'6"
Roof Framing	Truss
Exterior Walls	2×6

Please note: The photographed home may have been modified to suit homeowner preferences. If you order plans, have a builder or design professional check them against the photograph to confirm actual construction details.

SECOND FLOOR

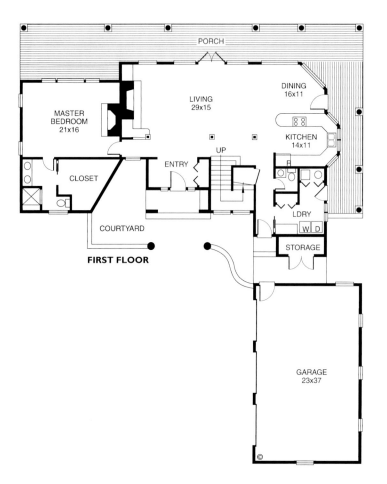

FIRST FLOOR

REAR ELEVATION

Design 66005

See Order Pages and Index for Info

Units	Single
Price Code	H
Total Finished	3,002 sq. ft.
First Finished	2,169 sq. ft.
Second Finished	833 sq. ft.
Bonus Unfinished	272 sq. ft.
Garage Unfinished	675 sq. ft.
Deck Unfinished	352 sq. ft.
Porch Unfinished	62 sq. ft.
Dimensions	65'x67'7"
Foundation	Slab
Bedrooms	4
Full Baths	2
3/4 Baths	1
Half Baths	1
First Ceiling	10'
Second Ceiling	8'
Max Ridge Height	29'
Roof Framing	Stick
Exterior Walls	2x4

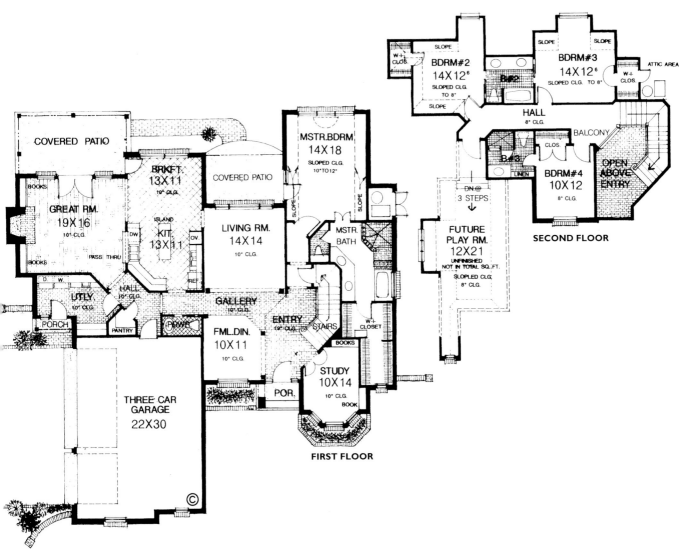

Design 66003

See Order Pages and Index for Info

Units	Single
Price Code	H
Total Finished	3,054 sq. ft.
First Finished	2,187 sq. ft.
Second Finished	867 sq. ft.
Bonus Unfinished	296 sq. ft.
Garage Unfinished	673 sq. ft.
Deck Unfinished	245 sq. ft.
Porch Unfinished	42 sq. ft.
Dimensions	66'10"×58'10"
Foundation	Basement
	Slab
Bedrooms	4
Full Baths	3
Half Baths	1
First Ceiling	10'
Second Ceiling	8'
Max Ridge Height	33'
Roof Framing	Stick
Exterior Walls	2×4

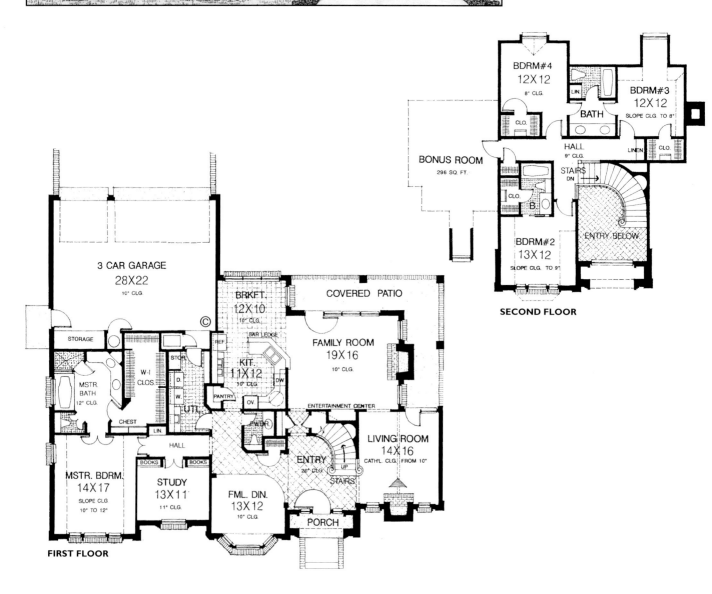

SECOND FLOOR

BDRM#4 12X12 — 8' CLG.
BDRM#3 12X12 — SLOPE CLG. TO 8'
BATH
LIN.
CLO.
HALL 9' CLG.
LINEN
CLO.
STAIRS DN
BONUS ROOM 296 SQ. FT.
CLO.
B
BDRM#2 13X12 — SLOPE CLG. TO 9'
ENTRY BELOW

FIRST FLOOR

3 CAR GARAGE 28X22 — 10' CLG.
STORAGE
MSTR. BATH 12' CLG.
W-I CLOS.
STOR.
REF
BRKFT. 12X10 — 10' CLG.
BAR LEDGE
KIT. 11X12 — 10' CLG.
COVERED PATIO
FAMILY ROOM 19X16 — 10' CLG.
D.
W.
DW
PANTRY
OV
UTL.
CHEST
LIN.
HALL
PWDR.
ENTERTAINMENT CENTER
ENTRY 20' CLG.
UP STAIRS
LIVING ROOM 14X16 — CATH'L. CLG. FROM 10'
MSTR. BDRM. 14X17 — SLOPE CLG 10' TO 12'
STUDY 13X11 — 11' CLG.
BOOKS
BOOKS
FML. DIN. 13X12 — 10' CLG.
PORCH

3,001-3,500 Sq. Ft.

SECOND FLOOR

Design 98596

See Order Pages and Index for Info

FIRST FLOOR

Units	Single
Price Code	H
Total Finished	3,062 sq. ft.
First Finished	2,115 sq. ft.
Second Finished	947 sq. ft.
Bonus Unfinished	195 sq. ft.
Garage Unfinished	635 sq. ft.
Deck Unfinished	210 sq. ft.
Porch Unfinished	32 sq. ft.
Dimensions	68'10"x58'1"
Foundation	Basement
	Crawlspace
	Slab
Bedrooms	4
Full Baths	2
3/4 Baths	1
Half Baths	1
Max Ridge Height	32'6"
Roof Framing	Stick
Exterior Walls	2x4

Design 57054

See Order Pages and Index for Info

PHOTOGRAPHY: COURTESY OF WILLIAM E. POOLE ARCHITECTS INC.

Hot New Design

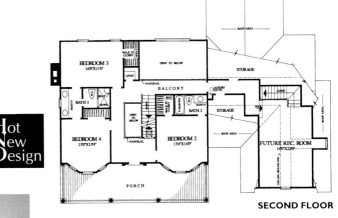

SECOND FLOOR

Units	Single
Price Code	Please call for pricing
Total Finished	3,057 sq. ft.
First Finished	1,995 sq. ft.
Second Finished	1,062 sq. ft.
Bonus Unfinished	459 sq. ft.
Dimensions	71'x57'4"
Foundation	Combo Basement/ Crawlspace
Bedrooms	4
Full Baths	2
3/4 Baths	1
Half Baths	1
Max Ridge Height	38'
Roof Framing	Stick
Exterior Walls	2x4

Please note: The photographed home may have been modified to suit homeowner preferences. If you order plans, have a builder or design professional check them against the photograph to confirm actual construction details.

FAMILY ROOM

FIRST FLOOR

Design 97400

See Order Pages and Index for Info

Units	Single
Price Code	H
Total Finished	3,094 sq. ft.
First Finished	2,112 sq. ft.
Second Finished	982 sq. ft.
Basement Unfinished	2,112 sq. ft.
Garage Unfinished	650 sq. ft.
Dimensions	67'1"x65'10⅛"
Foundation	Basement
	Slab
Bedrooms	4
Full Baths	3
Half Baths	1
First Ceiling	9'
Max Ridge Height	30'4"
Roof Framing	Stick
Exterior Walls	2x4

* Alternate foundation options available at an additional charge.
Please call 1-800-235-5700 for more information.

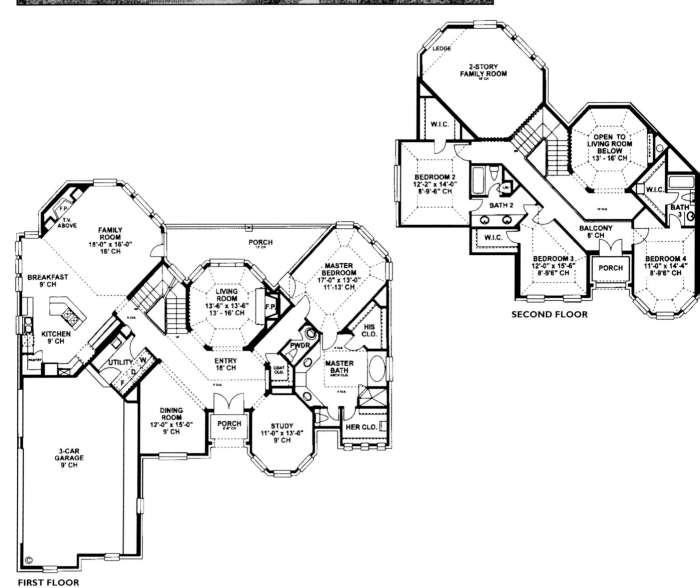

SECOND FLOOR

FIRST FLOOR

Design 92277

See Order Pages and Index for Info

Units	Single
Price Code	H
Total Finished	3,110 sq. ft.
First Finished	2,190 sq. ft.
Second Finished	920 sq. ft.
Garage Unfinished	624 sq. ft.
Dimensions	69'x53'10"
Foundation	Basement
	Slab
Bedrooms	4
Full Baths	2
3/4 Baths	1
Half Baths	1
First Ceiling	10'
Second Ceiling	8'
Max Ridge Height	29'
Roof Framing	Stick
Exterior Walls	2x4

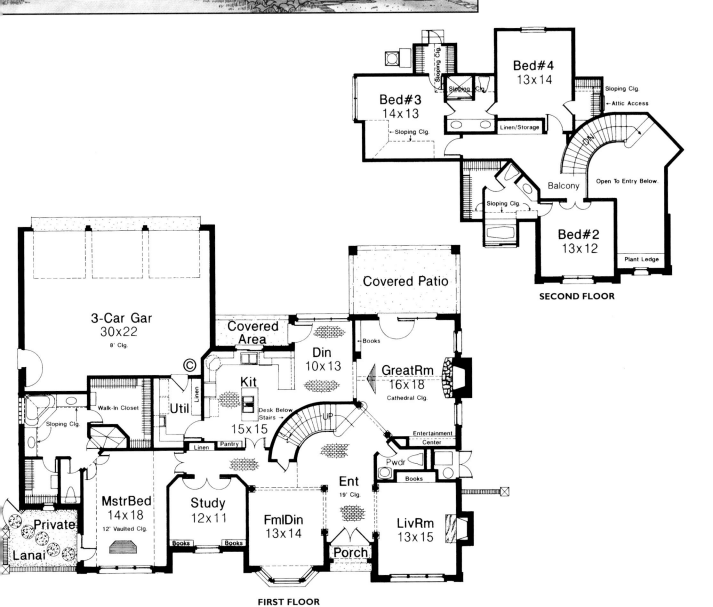

SECOND FLOOR

Bed#4 13x14

Bed#3 14x13
Sloping Clg.

Linen/Storage

Attic Access

Balcony

Open To Entry Below.

Bed#2 13x12

Plant Ledge

FIRST FLOOR

3-Car Gar 30x22
8' Clg.

Covered Area

Covered Patio

Din 10x13

Books

GreatRm 16x18
Cathedral Clg.

Walk-In Closet

Sloping Clg.

Util

Linen

Kit

Desk Below Stairs

15x15

UP

Entertainment Center

Linen Pantry

Pwdr

Books

Private Lanai

MstrBed 14x18
12' Vaulted Clg.

Study 12x11

Books Books

Ent 19' Clg.

FmlDin 13x14

Porch

LivRm 13x15

Books

Design **57058**

See Order Pages and Index for Info

Units	Single
Price Code	Please call for pricing
Total Finished	3,131 sq. ft.
First Finished	1,480 sq. ft.
Second Finished	1,651 sq. ft.
Dimensions	67'5"x61'5"
Foundation	Crawlspace
Bedrooms	4
Full Baths	2
Half Baths	1
Max Ridge Height	42'
Roof Framing	Stick
Exterior Walls	2x4

Hot New Design

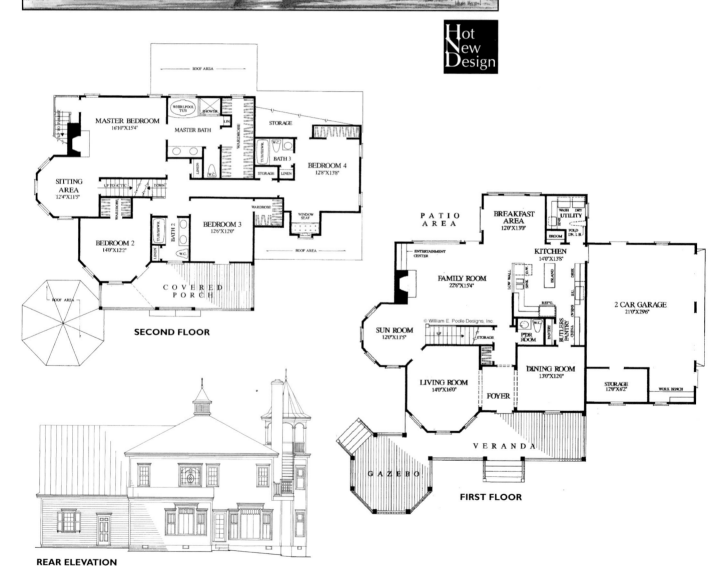

SECOND FLOOR

FIRST FLOOR

REAR ELEVATION

Design 94622

See Order Pages and Index for Info

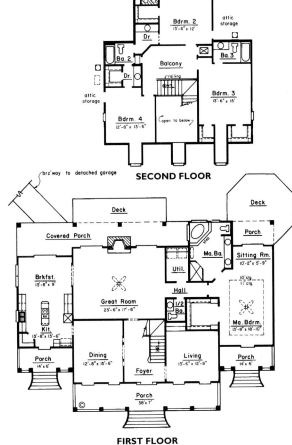

SECOND FLOOR

brz'way to detached garage

FIRST FLOOR

Units	Single
Price Code	H
Total Finished	3,149 sq. ft.
First Finished	2,033 sq. ft.
Second Finished	1,116 sq. ft.
Deck Unfinished	303 sq. ft.
Porch Unfinished	789 sq. ft.
Dimensions	66'x56'
Foundation	Slab
	Pier/Post
Bedrooms	4
Full Baths	3
Half Baths	1
First Ceiling	10'
Second Ceiling	9'
Max Ridge Height	33'
Roof Framing	Truss
Exterior Walls	2x4, 2x6

Design 98491

See Order Pages and Index for Info

SECOND FLOOR

FIRST FLOOR

Units	Single
Price Code	H
Total Finished	3,163 sq. ft.
First Finished	2,294 sq. ft.
Second Finished	869 sq. ft.
Bonus Unfinished	309 sq. ft.
Basement Unfinished	2,294 sq. ft.
Garage Unfinished	495 sq. ft.
Dimensions	63'6"x63'
Foundation	Basement
	Crawlspace
Bedrooms	4
Full Baths	3
Half Baths	1
Max Ridge Height	33'6"
Roof Framing	Stick
Exterior Walls	2x4

Design 10663

See Order Pages and Index for Info

PHOTOGRAPHY: JOHN EHRENCLOU

Units	Single
Price Code	H
Total Finished	3,176 sq. ft.
First Finished	2,310 sq. ft.
Second Finished	866 sq. ft.
Garage Unfinished	679 sq. ft.
Dimensions	78'x64'
Foundation	Basement
	Crawlspace
	Slab
Bedrooms	3
Full Baths	3
Half Baths	1
First Ceiling	10'
Second Ceiling	8'
Max Ridge Height	28'
Roof Framing	Stick
Exterior Walls	2x6

Please note: The photographed home may have been modified to suit homeowner preferences. If you order plans, have a builder or design professional check them against the photograph to confirm actual construction details.

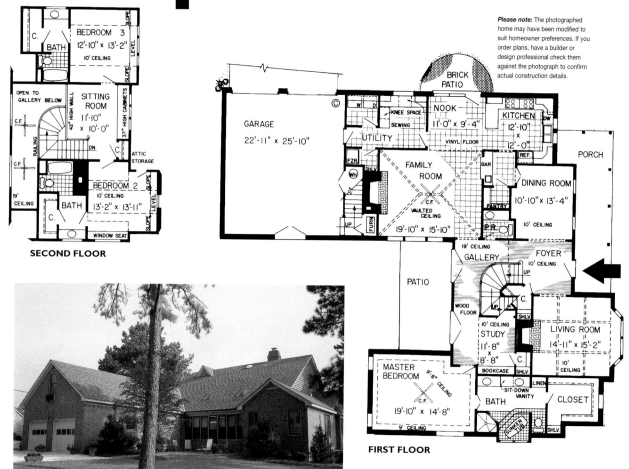

SECOND FLOOR

FIRST FLOOR

REAR ELEVATION

Design 57065

See Order Pages and Index for Info

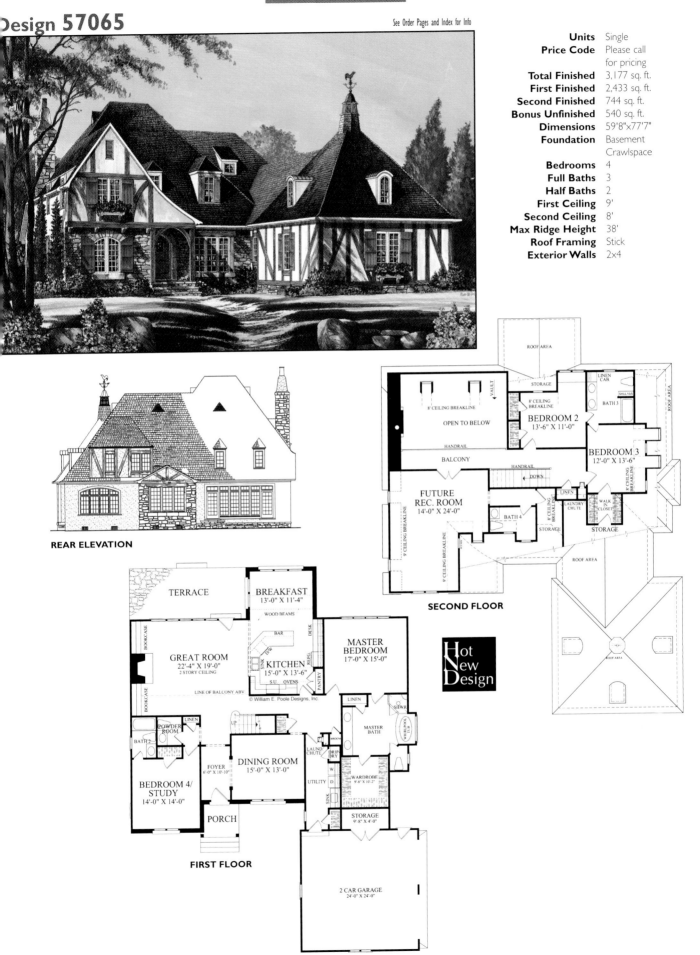

Units	Single
Price Code	Please call for pricing
Total Finished	3,177 sq. ft.
First Finished	2,433 sq. ft.
Second Finished	744 sq. ft.
Bonus Unfinished	540 sq. ft.
Dimensions	59'8"x77'7"
Foundation	Basement Crawlspace
Bedrooms	4
Full Baths	3
Half Baths	2
First Ceiling	9'
Second Ceiling	8'
Max Ridge Height	38'
Roof Framing	Stick
Exterior Walls	2x4

REAR ELEVATION

SECOND FLOOR

FIRST FLOOR

ROOF AREA

STORAGE

LINEN CAB

8' CEILING BREAKLINE

8' CEILING BREAKLINE

BATH 3

SHELVES

VAULT

OPEN TO BELOW

BEDROOM 2
13'-6" X 11'-0"

BEDROOM 3
12'-0" X 13'-6"

HANDRAIL

BALCONY

HANDRAIL

DOWN

FUTURE REC. ROOM
14'-0" X 24'-0"

LINEN

LAUNDRY CHUTE

WALK IN CLOSET

8' CEILING BREAKLINE

9' CEILING BREAKLINE

BATH 4

STORAGE

STORAGE

9' CEILING BREAKLINE

ROOF AREA

ROOF AREA

TERRACE

BREAKFAST
13'-0" X 11'-4"

WOOD BEAMS

BAR

DESK

GREAT ROOM
22'-4" X 19'-0"
2 STORY CEILING

SINK D.W.

KITCHEN
15'-0" X 13'-6"

REFG.

PANTRY

MASTER BEDROOM
17'-0" X 15'-0"

BOOKCASE

S.U. OVENS

LINE OF BALCONY ABV.

© William E. Poole Designs, Inc.

BOOKCASE

POWDER ROOM

LINEN

UP

LINEN

SHWR.

MASTER BATH

WHIRLPOOL

BATH 2

FOYER
6'-0" X 10'-10"

DINING ROOM
15'-0" X 13'-0"

LAUND. CHUTE

DRIP DRY

BEDROOM 4/ STUDY
14'-0" X 14'-0"

UTILITY

SINK

W.

D.

WARDROBE
9'-8" X 10'-2"

PORCH

STORAGE
9'-8" X 4'-0"

2 CAR GARAGE
24'-0" X 24'-0"

Hot New Design

3,001-3,500 Sq. Ft.

Design 98588

See Order Pages and Index for Info

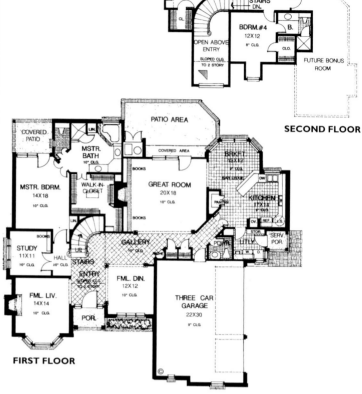

SECOND FLOOR

FIRST FLOOR

Units	Single
Price Code	H
Total Finished	3,219 sq. ft.
First Finished	2,337 sq. ft.
Second Finished	882 sq. ft.
Bonus Unfinished	357 sq. ft.
Garage Unfinished	640 sq. ft.
Deck Unfinished	240 sq. ft.
Porch Unfinished	120 sq. ft.
Dimensions	70'×63'2"
Foundation	Basement
	Slab
Bedrooms	4
Full Baths	2
3/4 Baths	2
Half Baths	1
Max Ridge Height	32'6"
Roof Framing	Stick
Exterior Walls	2x4

Design 98400

See Order Pages and Index for Info

CAD FILES AVAILABLE
For more information call
800-235-5700

SECOND FLOOR

FIRST FLOOR

Units	Single
Price Code	I
Total Finished	3,262 sq. ft.
First Finished	1,418 sq. ft.
Second Finished	1,844 sq. ft.
Basement Unfinished	1,418 sq. ft.
Garage Unfinished	820 sq. ft.
Dimensions	63'×41'
Foundation	Basement
	Crawlspace
Bedrooms	4
Full Baths	3
Half Baths	1
First Ceiling	9'
Second Ceiling	8'
Max Ridge Height	33'
Roof Framing	Stick
Exterior Walls	2x4

Design 98513

See Order Pages and Index for Info

Units	Single
Price Code	I
Total Finished	3,352 sq. ft.
Main Finished	3,352 sq. ft.
Garage Unfinished	672 sq. ft.
Deck Unfinished	462 sq. ft.
Porch Unfinished	60 sq. ft.
Dimensions	91'x71'9"
Foundation	Slab
Bedrooms	4
Full Baths	2
3/4 Baths	1
Half Baths	1
Main Ceiling	9'-11'
Max Ridge Height	28'2"
Roof Framing	Stick
Exterior Walls	2x4

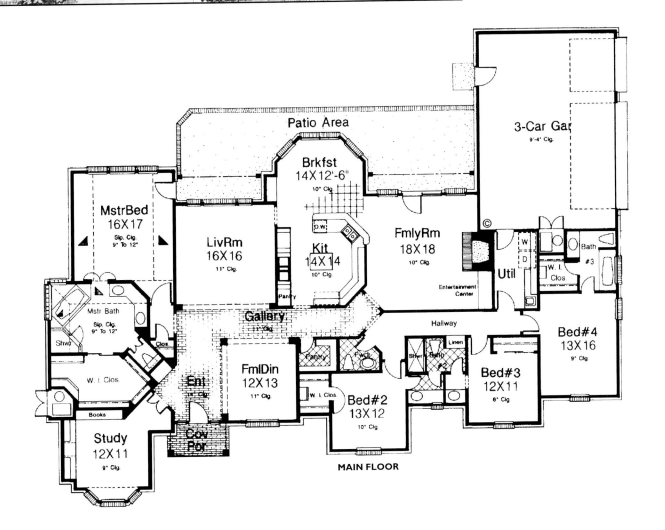

MAIN FLOOR

Design 57064

See Order Pages and Index for Info

Units	Single
Price Code	Please call for pricing
Total Finished	3,372 sq. ft.
First Finished	2,193 sq. ft.
Second Finished	1,179 sq. ft.
Bonus Unfinished	558 sq. ft.
Dimensions	63'4"x75'5"
Foundation	Combo Basement/ Crawlspace
Bedrooms	4
Full Baths	3
Half Baths	1
Max Ridge Height	32'
Roof Framing	Stick
Exterior Walls	2x4

REAR ELEVATION

Hot New Design

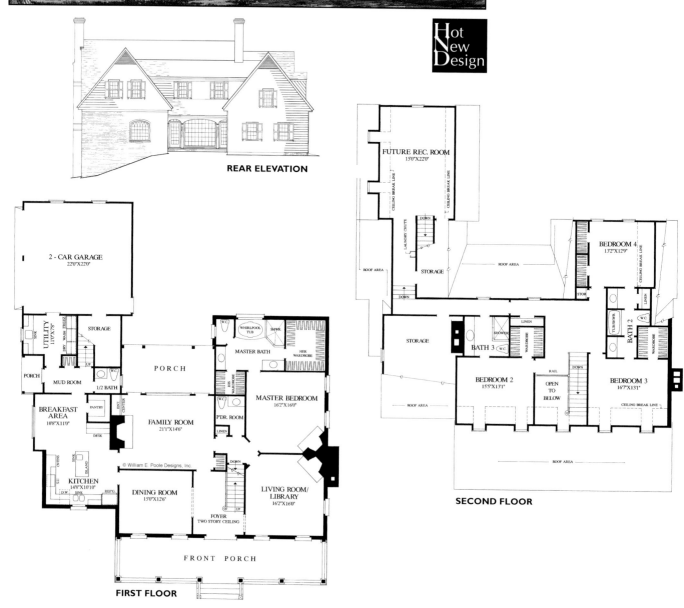

FUTURE REC. ROOM
15'0"X22'0"

STORAGE

STORAGE

BEDROOM 4
13'2"X12'9"

BATH 3

BEDROOM 2
15'5"X13'1"

OPEN TO BELOW

BATH 2

BEDROOM 3
16'7"X13'1"

SECOND FLOOR

2 - CAR GARAGE
22'0"X22'0"

UTILITY
11'0"X7'8"

STORAGE

PORCH

MUD ROOM

1/2 BATH

MASTER BATH

WHIRLPOOL TUB

SHWR.

HER WARDROBE

PORCH

MASTER BEDROOM
16'2"X16'0"

P'DR. ROOM

BREAKFAST AREA
10'8"X11'0"

PANTRY

FAMILY ROOM
21'1"X14'6"

DESK

© William E. Poole Designs, Inc.

KITCHEN
14'8"X10'10"

ISLAND

DINING ROOM
15'0"X12'6"

DOWN

LIVING ROOM/ LIBRARY
16'2"X16'0"

FOYER
TWO STORY CEILING

FRONT PORCH

FIRST FLOOR

Design 57062

See Order Pages and Index for Info

Units	Single
Price Code	Please call for pricing
Total Finished	3,408 sq. ft.
First Finished	2,216 sq. ft.
Second Finished	1,192 sq. ft.
Bonus Unfinished	458 sq. ft.
Dimensions	67'10"x56'
Foundation	Crawlspace
Bedrooms	4
Full Baths	3
Half Baths	1
Max Ridge Height	37'
Roof Framing	Stick
Exterior Walls	2x4

Hot New Design

REAR ELEVATION

FIRST FLOOR

SECOND FLOOR

3,001-3,500 SQ. FT.

Design 32036

See Order Pages and Index for Info

PHOTOGRAPHY: JIM HEDRICH

Units	Single
Price Code	I
Total Finished	3,423 sq. ft.
First Finished	1,868 sq. ft.
Second Finished	1,555 sq. ft.
Garage Unfinished	740 sq. ft.
Dimensions	67'x48'6"
Foundation	Basement
Bedrooms	4
Full Baths	2
3/4 Baths	I
Half Baths	I
First Ceiling	9'
Second Ceiling	8'
Max Ridge Height	32'
Roof Framing	Stick
Exterior Walls	2x4

Please note: The photographed home may have been modified to suit homeowner preferences. If you order plans, have a builder or design professional check them against the photograph to confirm actual construction details.

SECOND FLOOR

FIRST FLOOR

Design 63021

See Order Pages and Index for Info

PHOTOGRAPHY: COURTESY OF THE DESIGNER

Units	Single
Price Code	I
Total Finished	3,434 sq. ft.
Main Finished	3,434 sq. ft.
Bonus Unfinished	512 sq. ft.
Garage Unfinished	814 sq. ft.
Dimensions	82'4"x83'8"
Foundation	Slab
Bedrooms	5
Full Baths	3
3/4 Baths	I
Main Ceiling	10'-12'
Max Ridge Height	23'5"
Roof Framing	Truss

Please note: The photographed home may have been modified to suit homeowner preferences. If you order plans, have a builder or design professional check them against the photograph to confirm actual construction details.

BONUS

MAIN FLOOR

KITCHEN/FAMILY ROOM

Order on-line at www.familyhomeplans.com

Design 10534

See Order Pages and Index for Info

PHOTOGRAPHY: JOHN EHRENCLOU

Units	Single
Price Code	I
Total Finished	3,440 sq. ft.
First Finished	2,486 sq. ft.
Second Finished	954 sq. ft.
Basement Unfinished	2,486 sq. ft.
Garage Unfinished	576 sq. ft.
Dimensions	73'4"x60'4"
Foundation	Basement
	Crawlspace
	Slab
Bedrooms	4
Full Baths	2
3/4 Baths	I
Half Baths	I
Max Ridge Height	35'
Roof Framing	Stick
Exterior Walls	2x6

SECOND FLOOR

Please note: The photographed home may have been modified to suit homeowner preferences. If you order plans, have a builder or design professional check them against the photograph to confirm actual construction details.

REAR ELEVATION

FIRST FLOOR

Design 32606

See Order Pages and Index for Info

PHOTOGRAPHY: BETH SINGER

Units	Single
Price Code	I
Total Finished	3,474 sq. ft.
First Finished	2,569 sq. ft.
Second Finished	905 sq. ft.
Bonus Unfinished	401 sq. ft.
Basement Unfinished	2,522 sq. ft.
Garage Unfinished	680 sq. ft.
Dimensions	62'10"x74'7½"
Foundation	Basement
Bedrooms	3
Full Baths	3
Half Baths	1
First Ceiling	9'
Second Ceiling	8'
Max Ridge Height	40'
Roof Framing	Truss
Exterior Walls	2x6

Please note: The photographed home may have been modified to suit homeowner preferences. If you order plans, have a builder or design professional check them against the photograph to confirm actual construction details.

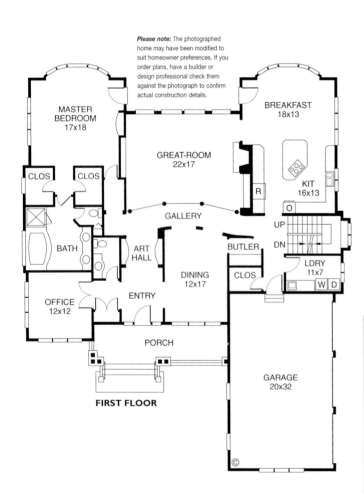

FIRST FLOOR

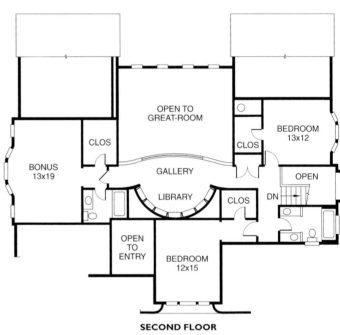

SECOND FLOOR

REAR ELEVATION

Design 32146

See Order Pages and Index for Info

Units	Single
Price Code	K
Total Finished	3,895 sq. ft.
First Finished	2,727 sq. ft.
Second Finished	1,168 sq. ft.
Bonus Unfinished	213 sq. ft.
Basement Unfinished	2,250 sq. ft.
Garage Unfinished	984 sq. ft.
Deck Unfinished	230 sq. ft.
Porch Unfinished	402 sq. ft.
Dimensions	73'8"x72'2"
Foundation	Basement
Bedrooms	5
Full Baths	4
Half Baths	1
First Ceiling	9'
Second Ceiling	8'
Vaulted Ceiling	22'
Max Ridge Height	43'
Roof Framing	Stick
Exterior Walls	2x6

PHOTOGRAPHY: RICK TAYLOR

ENTRY

Please note: The photographed home may have been modified to suit homeowner preferences. If you order plans, have a builder or design professional check them against the photograph to confirm actual construction details.

SECOND FLOOR

FIRST FLOOR

Over 3,500 Sq. Ft.

Design 98539

See Order Pages and Index for Info

Units	Single
Price Code	K
Total Finished	3,936 sq. ft.
First Finished	2,751 sq. ft.
Second Finished	1,185 sq. ft.
Bonus Unfinished	343 sq. ft.
Garage Unfinished	790 sq. ft.
Deck Unfinished	242 sq. ft.
Porch Unfinished	36 sq. ft.
Dimensions	79'x66'4"
Foundation	Basement
	Slab
Bedrooms	4
Full Baths	2
3/4 Baths	1
Half Baths	1
First Ceiling	10'
Max Ridge Height	35'
Roof Framing	Stick
Exterior Walls	2x4

Design 98590

See Order Pages and Index for Info

Units	Single
Price Code	L
Total Finished	4,166 sq. ft.
First Finished	3,168 sq. ft.
Second Finished	998 sq. ft.
Bonus Unfinished	320 sq. ft.
Garage Unfinished	810 sq. ft.
Deck Unfinished	290 sq. ft.
Porch Unfinished	180 sq. ft.
Dimensions	90'x63'5"
Foundation	Basement
	Crawlspace
	Slab
Bedrooms	4
Full Baths	3
Half Baths	1
First Ceiling	10'
Second Ceiling	9'
Max Ridge Height	36'
Roof Framing	Stick
Exterior Walls	2x4

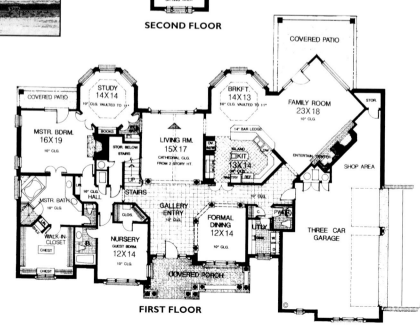

Design 32063

See Order Pages and Index for Info

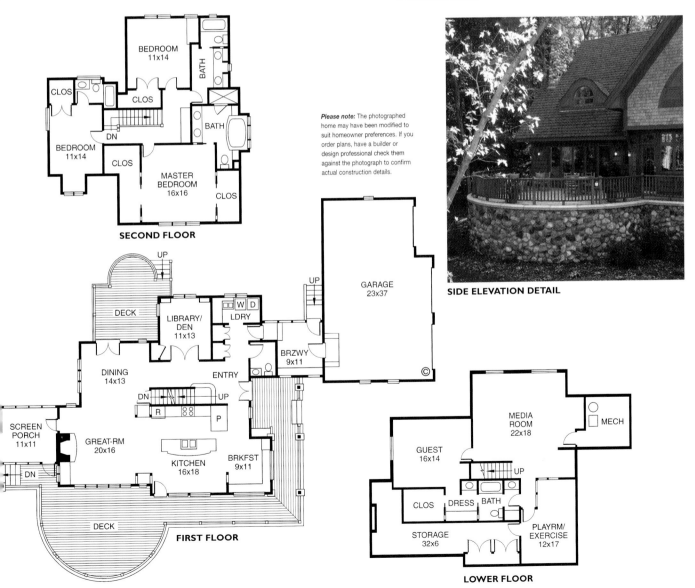

PHOTOGRAPHY: PHIL MUELLER

Units	Single
Price Code	L
Total Finished	4,283 sq. ft.
First Finished	1,642 sq. ft.
Second Finished	1,411 sq. ft.
Lower Finished	1,230 sq. ft.
Basement Unfinished	412 sq. ft.
Deck Unfinished	207 sq. ft.
Porch Unfinished	1,000 sq. ft.
Dimensions	92'x61'
Foundation	Basement
Bedrooms	4
Full Baths	4
Half Baths	1
First Ceiling	9'
Second Ceiling	8'
Max Ridge Height	35'
Roof Framing	Stick
Exterior Walls	2x6

SECOND FLOOR

- BEDROOM 11x14
- BATH
- CLOS
- CLOS
- BEDROOM 11x14
- CLOS
- DN
- BATH
- MASTER BEDROOM 16x16
- CLOS

Please note: The photographed home may have been modified to suit homeowner preferences. If you order plans, have a builder or design professional check them against the photograph to confirm actual construction details.

SIDE ELEVATION DETAIL

FIRST FLOOR

- DECK
- UP
- LIBRARY/DEN 11x13
- W D
- LDRY
- UP
- GARAGE 23x37
- BRZWY 9x11
- DINING 14x13
- ENTRY
- DN UP
- R
- P
- SCREEN PORCH 11x11
- GREAT-RM 20x16
- KITCHEN 16x18
- BRKFST 9x11
- DN
- DECK

LOWER FLOOR

- MEDIA ROOM 22x18
- MECH
- GUEST 16x14
- UP
- CLOS
- DRESS
- BATH
- STORAGE 32x6
- PLAYRM/EXERCISE 12x17

Design 32046

See Order Pages and Index for Info

PHOTOGRAPHY: RICK TAYLOR

Units	Single
Price Code	L
Total Finished	4,292 sq. ft.
First Finished	1,928 sq. ft.
Second Finished	2,364 sq. ft.
Garage Unfinished	578 sq. ft.
Deck Unfinished	532 sq. ft.
Porch Unfinished	329 sq. ft.
Dimensions	64'x65'
Foundation	Crawlspace
Bedrooms	5
Full Baths	4
Half Baths	I
First Ceiling	9'
Second Ceiling	8'
Max Ridge Height	33'
Roof Framing	Stick
Exterior Walls	2x4

*This home is not to be built in Hillsboro County, Fla.

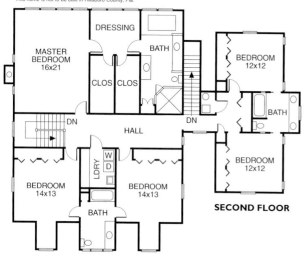

SECOND FLOOR

REAR ELEVATION

FIRST FLOOR

Please note: The photographed home may have been modified to suit homeowner preferences. If you order plans, have a builder or design professional check them against the photograph to confirm actual construction details.

Design 57060

Over 3,500 Sq. Ft.

See Order Pages and Index for Info

Units	Single
Price Code	Please call for pricing
Total Finished	4,293 sq. ft.
First Finished	2,913 sq. ft.
Second Finished	1,380 sq. ft.
Bonus Unfinished	905 sq. ft.
Dimensions	88'4"x100'8"
Foundation	Crawlspace
Bedrooms	4
Full Baths	3
3/4 Baths	1
Half Baths	1
Max Ridge Height	30'
Roof Framing	Stick
Exterior Walls	2x4

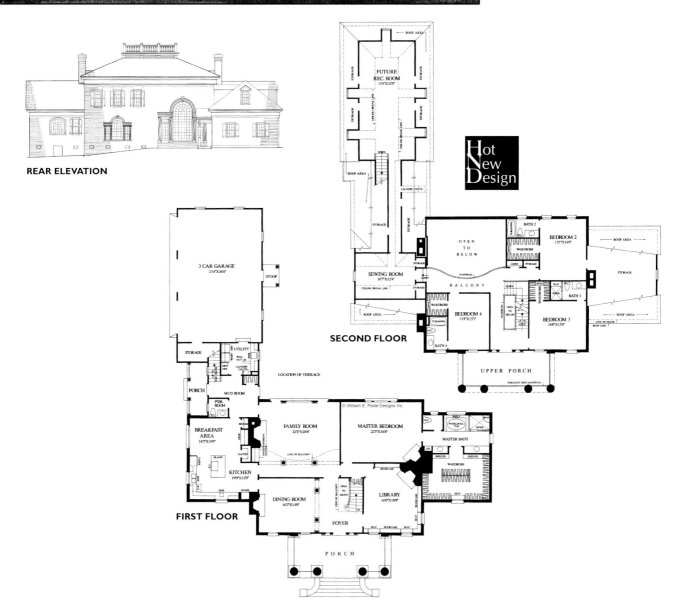

REAR ELEVATION

SECOND FLOOR

Hot New Design

FIRST FLOOR

© William E. Poole Designs Inc.

Design 32327

See Order Pages and Index for Info

PHOTOGRAPHY: JIM HENDRICH

Units	Single
Price Code	L
Total Finished	5,124 sq. ft.
First Finished	2,984 sq. ft.
Second Finished	2,140 sq. ft.
Garage Unfinished	815 sq. ft.
Deck Unfinished	691 sq. ft.
Porch Unfinished	327 sq. ft.
Dimensions	96'2"×58'8"
Foundation	Basement
Bedrooms	5
Full Baths	4
3/4 Baths	1
First Ceiling	9'
Second Ceiling	9'
Vaulted Ceiling	19'
Tray Ceiling	10'
Max Ridge Height	38'6"
Roof Framing	Truss
Exterior Walls	2x4, 2x6

REAR ELEVATION

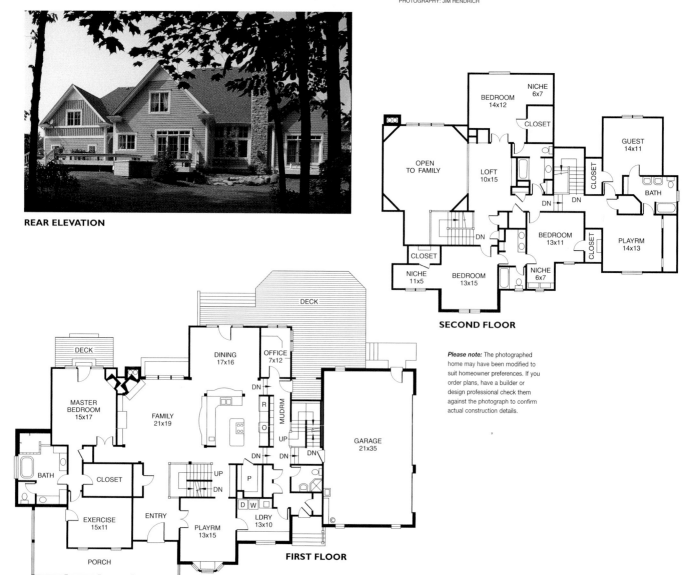

Please note: The photographed home may have been modified to suit homeowner preferences. If you order plans, have a builder or design professional check them against the photograph to confirm actual construction details.

SECOND FLOOR

FIRST FLOOR

Design 57061

See Order Pages and Index for Info

Units	Single
Price Code	Please call for pricing
Total Finished	5,795 sq. ft.
First Finished	3,712 sq. ft.
Second Finished	2,083 sq. ft.
Bonus Unfinished	409 sq. ft.
Dimensions	107'8"x59'
Foundation	Crawlspace
Bedrooms	5
Full Baths	4
3/4 Baths	1
Half Baths	3
Max Ridge Height	39'
Roof Framing	Stick
Exterior Walls	2x4

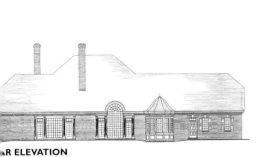

R ELEVATION

SECOND FLOOR

FIRST FLOOR

Important Information to Make Your Dream Come True

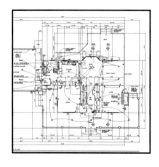

Detailed Floor Plans

The floor plans of your home accurately depict the dimensions of the positioning of all walls, doors, windows, stairs, and permanent fixtures. They will show you the relationship and dimensions of rooms, closets, and traffic patterns. The schematic of the electrical layout may be included in the plan.

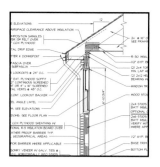

Typical Wall Section

This section will address insulation, roof components, and interior and exterior wall finishes. Your plans will be designed with either 2x4 or 2x6 exterior walls, but if you wish, most professional contractors can easily adapt the plans to the wall thickness you require.

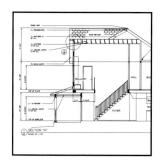

Typical Cross Section

A cut-away cross section throug the entire home shows your buildin contractor the exact correlation construction components at levels of the house. It will help clarify the load bearing points fro the roof all the way down to th basement. Available for most plan

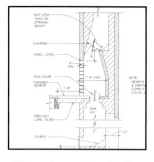

Fireplace Details

If the home you have chosen includes a fireplace, a fireplace detail will show typical methods of constructing the firebox, hearth, and flue chase for masonry units, or a wood frame chase for zero-clearance units. Available for most plans.

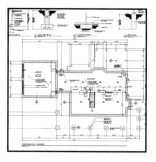

Foundation Plan

These plans will accurately show the dimensions of the footprint of your home, including load-bearing points and beam placement if applicable. The foundation style will vary from plan to plan. (Please note: There may be an additional charge for optional foundation plan. Please call for details.)

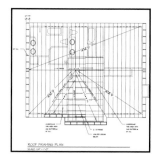

Roof Plan

The information necessary t construct the roof will be include with your home plans. Some plan will reference roof trusses, whil many others contain schemati framing plans. These framing plan will indicate the lumber sizes neces sary for the rafters and ridgeboard based on the designated roof loads

Exterior Elevations

These front, rear, and side views of the home include information pertaining to the exterior finish materials, roof pitches, and exterior height dimensions.

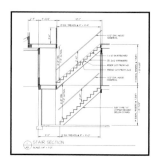

Stair Details

If the design you have chosen includes stairs, the plans will show the information that you need in order to build them-either through a stair cross section or on the floor plans.

Cabinet Plans

These plans, or in some cases elevations, will detail the layout of the kitchen and bathroom cabinets at a larger scale. Available for most plans.

Reversed Plans can Make Your Dream Home Just Right

You could have exactly the home you want by flipping it end-for-end. Simply order your plans "reversed." We'll send you one full set of mirror-image plans (with the writing backwards) as a master guide for you and your builder. The remaining sets of your order will come as shown in this book so the dimensions and specifications are easily read on the job site. Most plans in our collection will come stamped "reversed" so there is no confusion. We can only send reversed plans with multiple-set orders. There is a $50 charge for this service. Some plans in our collection are available in "Right Reading Reverse." Right Reading Reverse plans will show your home in reverse. This easy-to-read format will save you valuable time and money. Please contact our Sales Department at 800-235-5700 to check for Right Reading Reverse availability. There is a $135 charge for this service. **RRR**

Remember to Order Your Materials List

Available at a modest additional charge, the Materials List gives the quantity, dimensions, and specifications for the major materials needed to build your home. You will get faster, more accurate bids from your contractors and building suppliers and avoid paying for unused materials as well as waste. Materials Lists are available for all home plans except as otherwise indicated, but can only be ordered with a set of home plans. Due to differences in regional requirements and homeowner or builder preferences, electrical, plumbing and heating/air conditioning equipment specifications are not designed specifically for each plan. **ML**

What Garlinghouse Offers

Home Plan Blueprint Package

By purchasing a multiple-set package of blueprints or a Vellum from Garlinghouse, you not only receive the physical blueprint documents necessary for construction, but you are also granted a license to build one (and only one) home. You can also make simple modifications, including minor non-structural changes and material substitutions, to our design as long as these changes are made directly on the blueprints purchased from Garlinghouse and no additional copies are made.

Home Plan Vellums

By purchasing Vellums for one of our home plans, you receive the same construction drawings found in the blueprints, but printed on vellum paper. Vellums can be erased and are perfect for making design changes. They are also semi-transparent, making them easy to duplicate. But most importantly, the purchase of home plan Vellums comes with a broader license that allows you to make changes to the design (i.e., create a hand drawn or CAD derivative work), to make copies of the plan, and to build one home from the plan.

License to Build Additional Homes

With the purchase of a blueprint package or Vellums, you automatically receive a license to build one home and only one home. If you want to build more homes than you are licensed to build through your purchase of a plan, then additional licenses must be purchased at reasonable costs from Garlinghouse. Inquire for more information.

Modifying Your Design Easily

How to Modify Your Garlinghouse Home Plan

Simple modifications to your dream home, including minor non-structural changes and material substitutions, can be made by you and your builder with the consent of your local building official, by marking the changes directly on your blueprints. However, if you are considering making significant changes to your chosen design, we recommend that you use the services of The Garlinghouse Design Staff. We will help take your ideas and turn them into a reality, just the way you want.

Here's our procedure:
Call 800-235-5700 and order your modification estimate. The fee for this estimate is $50. We will review your plan changes and provide you with an estimate to draft your specific modifications before you purchase the vellums. **Please note: A vellum must be purchased to modify a home plan design.** After you receive your estimate, if you decide to have Garlinghouse do the changes, the $50 estimate fee will be deducted from the cost of your modifications. If, however, you chose to use a different service, the $50 estimate fee is non-refundable. **(Note: Personal checks cannot be accepted for the estimate.)**

A 75% deposit is required before we begin making the actual modifications to your plans.

Once the design changes have been completed to your vellum plan, a representative will call to inform you that your modified vellum plan is complete and will be shipped as soon as the final payment has been made. For additional information, call us at 1-800-235-5700. Please refer to the Modification Pricing Guide for estimated modification costs.

Reproducible Vellums for Local Modification Ease

If you decide not to use Garlinghouse for your modifications, we recommend that you follow our same procedure of purchasing vellums. You then have the option of using the services of the original designer of the plan, a local professional designer, or an architect to make the modifications.

With a vellum copy of our plans, a design professional can alter the drawings just the way you want, then you can print as many copies of the modified plans as you need to build your house. And, since you have already started with our complete detailed plans, the cost of those expensive professional services will be significantly less than starting from scratch. Refer to the price schedule for vellum costs.

IGNORING COPYRIGHT LAWS CAN BE A $100,000 MISTAKE

What You Can't Do
U.S. copyright laws allow for statutory penalties of up to $100,000 per incident for copyright infringement involving any of the copyrighted plans found in this publication. The law can be confusing. So, for your own protection, take the time to understand what you can and cannot do when it comes to home plans.

You Cannot Duplicate Home Plans
Purchasing a set of blueprints and making additional sets by reproducing the original is illegal. If you need more than one set of a particular home plan, you must purchase them.

You Cannot Copy Any Part of a Home Plan to Create Another
Creating your own plan by copying even part of a home design found in this publication without permission is called "creating a derivative work" and is illegal.

You Cannot Build a Home Without a License
You must have specific permission or a license to build a home from a copyrighted design, even if the finished home has been changed from the original plan. It is illegal to build one of the homes found in this publication without a license.

MODIFICATION PRICING GUIDE

The average prices shown below represent the most common requested changes. Prices for changes will vary depending on number of modifications requested, the house size, quality of original plan, format provided and method of design used by the original designer. Typically, modifications cost around $1500, excluding price of the (hand-drawn or computer generated) vellum.

Please contact us to get your $50 estimate at: 1-800-235-5700

CATEGORIES	AVERAGE CO
Adding or removing living space (square footage)	Quote required
Adding or removing a garage	Starting at $400
Garage: Front entry to side load or vice versa	Starting at $300
Adding a screened porch	Starting at $280
Adding a bonus room in the attic	Starting at $450
Changing full basement to crawlspace or vice versa	Starting at $495
Changing full basement to slab or vice versa	Starting at $495
Changing exterior building materials	Starting at $200
Changing roof lines	Starting at $360
Adjusting ceiling height	Starting at $280
Adding, moving or removing an exterior opening	$65 per opening
Adding or removing a fireplace	Starting at $90
Modifying a non-bearing wall or room	$65 per room
Changing exterior walls from 2"x4" to 2"x6"	Starting at $200
Redesigning a bathroom or a kitchen	Starting at $120
Reverse plan right reading	Quote required
Adapting plans for local building code requirements	Quote required
Engineering and Architectural stamping and services	Quote required
Adjust plan for handicapped accessibility	Quote required
Interactive Illustrations (choices of exterior materials)	Quote required
Metric conversion of home plan	Starting at $400

Detail Plans

Information on Construction Techniques—NOT PLAN SPECIFIC

PLEASE NOTE: The detail plans are not specific to any one home plan and should be used only as a general reference guide.

Because local codes and requirements vary greatly, we recommend that you obtain drawings and bids from licensed contractors to do your mechanical plans. However, if you want to know more about techniques—and deal more confidently with subcontractors—we offer these remarkably useful detail sheets. These detail sheets will aid in your understanding of these technical subjects.

$19.95 per set *(includes postage)*

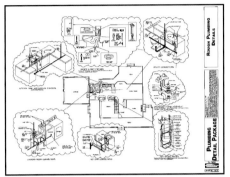
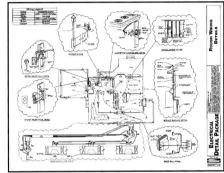

Residential Construction Details

Ten sheets that cover the essentials of stick-built residential home construction. Details foundation options—poured concrete basement, concrete block, or monolithic concrete slab. Shows all aspects of floor, wall and roof framing. Provides details for roof dormers, overhangs, chimneys and skylights. Conforms to requirements of Uniform Building code or BOCA code. Includes a quick index and a glossary of terms.

Residential Plumbing Details

Eight sheets packed with information detailing pipe installation methods, fittings, and sized. Details plumbing hook-ups for toilets, sinks, washers, sump pumps, and septic system construction. Conforms to requirements of National Plumbing code. Color coded with a glossary of terms and quick index.

Residential Electrical Details

Eight sheets that cover all aspects of residential wiring, from simple switch wiring to service entrance connections. Details distribution panel layout with outlet and switch schematics, circuit breaker and wiring installation methods, and ground fault interrupter specifications. Conforms to requirements of National Electrical Code. Color coded with a glossary of terms.

Your Blueprints Can Be Sealed by a Registered Architect

We can have your home plan blueprints sealed by an architect that is registered in most states. Please call our Order Department for details. Although an architect's seal will not guarantee approval of your home plan blueprints, a seal is sometimes required by your state or local building department in order to get a building permit. Please talk to your local building officials, before you order your blueprints, to determine if a seal is needed in your area. You will need to provide the county and state of your building site when ordering an architect's seal on your blueprints, and please allow additional time to process your order (an additional five to fifteen working days, at least). **Seals are available for plans numbered 0-15,999; 17,000-18,999; 20,000 - 31,999; and 34,000 - 34,999.**

State Energy Certificates

A few states require that an energy certificate be prepared for your new home to their specifications before a building permit can be issued. Again, your local building official can tell you if one is required in your state. You will first need to fill out the energy certificate checklist available to you when your order is placed. This list contains questions about type of heating used, siding, windows, location of home, etc. This checklist provides all the information needed to prepare your state energy certificate. **Please note: energy certificates are only available on orders for blueprints with an architect's seal. Certificates are available for plans numbered 0-15,999; 17,000-18,999; 20,000 - 31,999; and 34,000 - 34,999.**

Specifications & Contract Form

We send this form to you free of charge with your home plan order. The form is designed to be filled in by you or your contractor with the exact materials to use in the construction of your new home. Once signed by you and your contractor it will provide you with peace of mind throughout the construction process.

Questions?

Call our customer service department 1-800-235-5700.

CUSTOMER SERVICE

Questions on existing orders?

1-800-895-3715

To order your plan on-line
using our secure server, visit:
www.familyhomeplans.com

TO PLACE ORDERS

- **To order your home plans**
- **Questions about a plan**

1-800-235-5700

Order Code No. H5CAH

____ Set(s) of blueprints for plan #_____ $_____

____ Vellum for plan #_____ $_____

____ Foundation _____ $_____

____ Additional set(s) @ $50 each for plan #_____ $_____
(Not available for 1 set-study set)

____ Mirror Image Reverse @ $50 each $_____

____ Right Reading Reverse @ $135 each $_____

____ Materials list for plan #_____ $_____

____ Detail Plans *(Not plan specific)* @ $19.95 each

   ❏ Construction ❏ Plumbing ❏ Electrical $_____

____ Bottom-Line Zip Quote @ $29.95 for plan #_____ $_____

____ Additional Bottom-Line Zip Quotes

   @ $14.95 for plan(s) #_____ $_____

   Zip code where building _____

____ Itemized Zip Quote for plan(s) #_____ $_____

   Shipping $_____

   Subtotal $_____

   Sales Tax *(VA residents add 4.5%. Not required for other states.)* $_____

TOTAL AMOUNT ENCLOSED $_____

Send your check, money order, or credit card information to:
(No C.O.D.'s Please) *Prices subject to change without notice.*

Please submit all United States & other nations orders to:
The Garlinghouse Company
Attn: Order Fulfillment Dept.
4125 Lafayette Center Drive, Suite 100
Chantilly, VA 20151
CALL: (800) 235-5700   FAX: (703) 222-9705

Credit Card Information

Charge To: ❏ Mastercard ❏ Visa ❏ American Express ❏ Discov

Card # |_|_|_|_|_|_|_|_|_|_|_|_|_|_|_|_|_|_|_|

Signature _____ Exp. _____ / _____

Please Submit all Canadian plan orders to:
The Garlinghouse Company
102 Ellis Street
Penticton, BC V2A 4L5
CALL: (800) 361-7526   FAX: (250) 493-7526

Payment must be made in U.S. funds. Foreign Mail Orders: Certified bank checks in U.S. funds only

TERMS OF SALE FOR HOME PLANS: All home plans sold through this publication are copyright protected. Reproduction of these home plans, either in whole or in part, including any direct copying and/or preparation of derivative works thereof, for any reason without the prior written permission of Garlinghouse, LLC, is strictly prohibited. The purchase of a set of home plans in no way transfers a copyright or other ownership interest in it to the buyer except for a limited license to use that set of home plans for the construction of one, and only one, dwelling unit. The purchase of additional sets of that home plan at a reduced price from the original set or as a part of a multiple-set package does not entitle the buyer with a license to construct more than one dwelling unit.

Name: _____

Street: _____

City: _____

State: _____ Zip Code: _____

Daytime Phone: _____

Email Address: _____

Privacy Statement (please read)

Dear Valued Garlinghouse Customer,

Your privacy is extremely important to us. We'd like to take a little of your time to explain our privacy policy.

   As a service to you, we would like to provide your name to companies such as the following:

- Building material manufacturers that we are affiliated with, who would like to keep you current with their product line and specials.
- Building material retailers that would like to offer you competitive prices to help you save money.
- Financing companies that would like to offer you competitive mortgage rates.

   In addition, as our valued customer, we would like to send you newsletters to assist in your building experience. We would also appreciate your feedback by filling out a customer service survey aimed to improve our operations.

   You have total control over the use of your contact information. You let us know exactly how you want to be contacted.

(Please check all boxes that apply.)

   ☐ Don't mail
   ☐ Don't call
   ☐ Don't E-mail
   ☐ Only send Garlinghouse newsletters and customer service surveys

   In closing, we hope this shows Garlinghouse's firm commitment to providing superior customer service and protection of your privacy. We thank you for your time and consideration.

Sincerely,

The Garlinghouse Company

Blueprint Order Information

arlinghouse 2005 Blueprint Price Code Schedule
es subject to change without notice.

e Code	1 Set Study Set	4 Sets	8 Sets	Vellums	Materials List	Bottom-Line ZIP Quote
A	$395	$435	$485	$600	$60	$29.95
B	$425	$465	$515	$630	$60	$29.95
C	$450	$490	$540	$665	$60	$29.95
D	$490	$530	$580	$705	$60	$29.95
E	$530	$570	$620	$750	$70	$29.95
F	$585	$625	$675	$800	$70	$29.95
G	$630	$670	$720	$850	$70	$29.95
H	$675	$715	$765	$895	$70	$29.95
I	$700	$740	$790	$940	$80	$29.95
J	$740	$780	$830	$980	$80	$29.95
K	$805	$845	$895	$1,020	$80	$29.95
L	$825	$865	$915	$1,055	$80	$29.95

Additional sets with original order $50

Shipping — (Plans 1-35999)

	1-3 Sets	4-6 Sets	7+ & Vellums
Standard Delivery (UPS 2-Day)	$25.00	$30.00	$35.00
Overnight Delivery	$35.00	$40.00	$45.00

Shipping — (Plans 36000-99999)

	1-3 Sets	4-6 Sets	7+ & Vellums
Ground Delivery (7-10 Days)	$15.00	$20.00	$25.00
Express Delivery (3-5 Days)	$20.00	$25.00	$30.00

International Shipping & Handling

	1-3 Sets	4-6 Sets	7+ & Vellums
Regular Delivery Canada (10-14 Days)	$30.00	$35.00	$40.00
Express Delivery Canada (7-10 Days)	$60.00	$70.00	$80.00
Overseas Delivery Airmail (3-4 Weeks)	$50.00	$60.00	$65.00

For Our USA Customers:
Order Toll Free: 1-800-235-5700
Mon.- Fri. 8:00 a.m. - 8:00 p.m. EST.
Sat. 10:00 a.m. - 4:00 p.m. EST.
FAX your Credit Card order to 1-703-222-9705
All foreign residents (except Canada) call 1-703-547-4154

TO PLACE ORDERS
• To order your home plans
• Questions about a plan
1-800-235-5700

CUSTOMER SERVICE
Questions on existing orders?
1-800-895-3715

For Our Canadian Customers:
Order Toll Free: 1-800-361-7526
Mon.-Fri. 8:00 a.m. to 5:00 p.m. PST.
or FAX your Credit Card order to 1-250-493-7526
Customer Service: 1-250-493-0942

Please have ready: 1. Your credit card number 2. The plan number 3. The order code number **H5CAH**

Before ordering, please read all ordering information.

ow Many Sets of Plans Will You Need?

e Standard 8-Set Construction Package

r experience shows that you'll speed up every step of construction d avoid costly building errors by ordering enough sets to go around. ch tradesperson wants a set—the general contractor and all sub-ntractors: foundation, electrical, plumbing, heating/air conditioning, d framers. Don't forget your lending institution, building department, d, of course, a set for yourself. * Recommended For Construction *

e Minimum 4-Set Construction Package

ou're comfortable with arduous follow-up, this package can save u a few dollars by giving you the option of passing down plan sets as rk progresses. You might have enough copies to go around if work es exactly as scheduled and no plans are lost or damaged by sub-ntractors. But for only $60 more, the 8-set package eliminates these rries. * Recommended For Bidding *

e 1 Set-Study Set

e offer this set so you can study the blueprints to plan your dream me in detail. They are stamped "study set only—not for construction" d you cannot build a home from them. In pursuant to copyright laws, s illegal to reproduce any blueprint. 1 set-study sets cannot be dered in a reversed format.

Reorder, Call 800-235-5700

ou find after your initial purchase that you require additional sets of ns, a materials list, or other items, you may purchase them from us at ecial reorder prices (please call for pricing details) provided that you order within six months of your original order date. There is a $28 order processing fee that is charged on all reorders. For more ormation on reordering plans, please contact our Sales Department.

n Important Note About ilding Code Requirements

plans are drawn to conform to one or more of the industry's major tional building standards. However, due to the variety of local lding regulations, your plan may need to be modified to comply with al requirements—snow loads, energy loads, seismic zones, etc. Do eck them fully and consult your local building officials. A few states quire that all building plans used be drawn by an architect registered hat state. While having your plans reviewed and stamped by such architect may be prudent, laws requiring non-conforming plans like rs to be completely redrawn forces you to unnecessarily pay very

large fees. If your state has such a law, we strongly recommend you contact your state representative to protest. The rendering, floor plans, and technical information contained within this publication are not guaranteed to be totally accurate. Consequently, no information from this publication should be used either as a guide to constructing a home or for estimating the cost of building a home. Complete blueprints must be purchased for such purposes.

Customer Service/Exchanges Call 800-895-3715

If for some reason you have a question about your existing order, please call 800-895-3715. Your plans are custom printed especially for you once you place your order. For that reason we cannot accept any returns. If for some reason you find that the plan you have purchased from us does not meet your needs, then you may exchange that plan for any other plan in our collection. We allow you 60 days from your original invoice date to make an exchange. At the time of the exchange, you will be charged a processing fee of 20% of the total amount of your original order, plus the difference in price between the plans (if applicable), plus the cost to ship the new plans to you. Call our Customer Service Department for more information. Please Note: Reproducible Vellums can only be exchanged if they are unopened.

Important Shipping Information

Please refer to the shipping charts on the order form for service availability for your specific plan number. Our delivery service must have a street address or Rural Route Box number—never a post office box. (PLEASE NOTE: Supplying a P.O. Box number will only will delay the shipping of your order.) Use a work address if no one is home during the day. Orders being shipped to APO or FPO must go via First Class Mail. Please include the proper postage. For our International Customers, only Certified bank checks and money orders are accepted and must be payable in U.S. currency. For speed, we ship international orders Air Parcel Post. Please refer to the chart for the correct shipping cost.

Important Canadian Shipping Information

To our friends in Canada, we have a plan design affiliate in Penticton, BC. This relationship will help you avoid the delays and charges associated with shipments from the United States. Moreover, our affiliate is familiar with the building requirements in your community and country. We prefer payments in U.S. currency. Please call our Canadian office at toll free 1-800-361-7526 for current Canadian prices.

Home Plan Index

Option Key

BL Bottom-Line Zip Quote	**ML** Materials List	**ZIP** Itemized Zip Quote	**RRR** Right Reading Reverse	**DUP** Duplex	

Plan	Pg.	Price Code	Options	Plan	Pg.	Price Code	Options	Plan	Pg.	Price Code	Options
10220	20	A	BL/ML	51004	23	A	BL	91026	40	A	BL/ML
10515	114	D	BL/ML/ZIP	52015	38	A	BL/ML	91595	103	L	
10534	191	I	BL/ML	55014	23	A	BL	92220	82	C	BL/ML/ZIP
10663	184	H	BL/ML	55024	156	E	BL	92277	181	H	BL
10690	134	E	BL/ML/ZIP	57000	118	*	BL	92421	93	C	BL/ML
10785	86	C	BL/ML/ZIP	57002	144	*	BL	92426	28	A	BL/ML
10839	77	B	BL/ML/ZIP/RRR	57003	143	*	BL	92576	172	G	BL/ML
19182	106	L	ML	57004	140	*	BL	92610	122	D	BL/ZIP
19299	92	C	BL/ML	57007	142	*	BL	92642	119	D	BL
19410	125	D	BL/ML/ZIP	57009	132	*	BL	92649	14	B	BL/ML
19422	74	B	BL/ML/ZIP	57031	64	*	BL	93209	157	E	BL/ML
19984	17	A	BL/ML	57054	179	*	BL	93212	121	D	BL/ML/ZIP
20083	68	B	BL/ML/ZIP	57056	163	*	BL	94260	117	F	BL/ML
20100	76	B	BL/ML/ZIP/RRR	57057	90	*	BL	94307	19	A	BL
20137	37	E	BL/ML	57058	182	*	BL	94622	183	H	BL
20156	41	A	BL/ML/ZIP/RRR	57059	171	*	BL	94676	108	D	BL
20161	37	A	BL/ML/ZIP	57060	197	*		94904	95	C	BL/ML/ZIP
20179	124	D	BL/ML/ZIP/RRR	57061	199	*		94938	71	B	
20198	67	C	BL/ML/ZIP	57062	189	*	BL	94941	160	D	BL/ML
20220	67	B	BL/ML/ZIP	57063	115	*	BL	96505	118	D	BL/ML
20501	87	C	BL/ML/ZIP	57064	188	*	BL	96506	72	B	BL/ML
24245	10	D	BL/ML/ZIP	57065	185	*	BL	96509	46	A	BL/ML
24262	141	E	BL/ML/ZIP	57072	133	*	BL	96513	71	B	BL/ML
24302	27	A	BL/ML/ZIP	57075	139	*	BL/ML	96529	121	D	BL/ML
24400	91	C	BL/ML/ZIP/RRR	57076	169	*	BL	97219	132	D	BL
24403	164	F	BL/ML/ZIP	57080	130	*	BL	97220	173	G	BL
24610	80	C	BL/ML/ZIP	57093	85	*	BL	97246	136	E	BL
24653	161	F	BL/ML/ZIP	57094	120	*	BL	97254	73	B	BL
24700	61	A	BL/ML/ZIP	60137	154	L		97274	44	A	BL/ML
24701	69	B	BL/ML/ZIP	61093	21	A		97313	172	G	BL
24706	47	A	BL/ML/ZIP	62006	165	F	BL	97400	180	H	BL/RRR
24711	45	A	BL/ML	62082	105	L		97757	77	B	BL
24714	79	C	BL/ML	63021	190	I	BL	97857	137	E	BL
24717	70	B	BL/ML/ZIP	65001	47	A	BL/ML	97946	165	F	BL
24721	66	B	BL/ML/ZIP	65003	26	A	BL/ML	98400	186	I	BL/ML
32003	152	D	BL	65004	135	E	BL/ML	98411	41	A	BL/ML
32018	17	A	BL	65005	25	A	BL/ML	98415	44	A	BL/ML/ZIP
32036	190	I	BL/ML/ZIP	65006	22	A	BL/ML	98425	84	C	BL/ML
32046	196	L	BL/ML/ZIP	65011	29	A	BL/ML	98426	162	F	BL/ML
32056	54	D	BL/ML	65014	33	A	BL/ML	98427	116	D	BL/ML
32063	195	L	ML/RRR	65018	20	B		98434	39	A	BL/ML
32109	115	D	BL/ML/ZIP	65026	25	C	BL/ML/DUP	98435	88	C	BL/ML
32114	146	K	BL/ML	65033	28	A	BL/ML	98441	65	B	BL
32122	56	A	BL/ML	65134	42	A		98447	124	D	BL/ML
32146	193	K	BL/ML/ZIP	65138	127	D	BL	98455	138	E	BL/ML
32192	35	A	BL	65140	30	A		98456	75	B	BL/ML
32209	52	B	BL/ML	65161	46	A		98458	174	G	BL/ML
32229	50	B	BL	65162	18	A	BL/ML	98464	80	C	BL/ML
32291	58	C	BL	65173	32	A		98466	126	D	BL
32323	35	A	BL	65234	93	E		98491	183	H	BL
32327	198	L		65242	34	A	BL	98494	167	G	BL
32353	176	G	BL	65263	19	A	BL/ML	98513	187	I	BL
32358	98	I	BL	65284	31	A		98528	166	F	BL/ZIP
32375	100	L		65368	94	C	BL/ML	98534	175	G	BL/ZIP
32387	128	D	BL	65380	81	C		98536	169	I	BL/ZIP
32400	170	G	BL	65387	24	A	BL/ML	98539	194	K	BL/ZIP
32427	148	K	BL	65642	21	A		98581	168	G	BL
32436	62	A	BL	66003	178	H	BL	98588	186	H	BL
32606	192	I	BL/ML/ZIP	66005	177	H	BL	98590	194	L	
34029	72	B	BL/ML/ZIP/RRR	68162	129	E	BL/ML	98596	179	H	BL
34031	83	C	BL/ML/ZIP	69030	22	A	BL	99115	89	C	BL/RRR
34043	69	B	BL/ML/ZIP/RRR	82003	39	A	BL	99431	145	E	BL/ML
34150	48	A	BL/ML/ZIP/RRR	82020	49	C	BL	99457	131	E	BL/ML
34600	38	A	BL/ML/ZIP/RRR	90048	36	A	BL/ML	99649	151	H	BL/ML
34601	43	A	BL/ML/ZIP/RRR	90443	166	G	BL/ML	99690	60	A	BL
34602	66	B	BL/ML/ZIP	90454	127	D	BL/ML	99693	158	F	BL/ML
34901	78	C	BL/ML/ZIP/RRR	90934	18	A	BL/ML	99696	150	D	BL/ML

*Please call 1-800-235-5700 for pricing information.

Order on-line at www.familyhomeplans.com

How Does Zip Quote Work?

Obtaining a Construction Cost Calculation Based on Labor Rates and Building Material Costs in Your Zip Code Area.

When you call to order, you must choose from the options available for your specific home in order for us to process your order. Once we receive your Zip Quote order, we process your specific home plan building materials list through our Home Cost Calculator which contains up-to-date rates for all residential labor trades and building material costs in your zip code area. The result?

A calculated cost to build your dream home in your zip code area. This calculation will help you (as a consumer or a builder) evaluate your building budget. All database information for our calculations is furnished by Marshall & Swift, L.P. For over 60 years, Marshall & Swift L.P. has been a leading provider of cost data to professionals in all aspects of the construction and remodeling industries.

Itemized Zip Quote

Option 1

The Itemized Zip Quote is a detailed building materials list. Each building materials list line item will separately state the labor cost, material cost, and equipment cost (if applicable) for the use of that building material in the construction process. This building materials list will be summarized by the individual building categories and will have additional columns where you can enter data from your contractor's estimates for a cost comparison between the different suppliers and contractors who will actually quote you their products and services. The price of your Itemized Zip Quote is based upon the pricing schedule of the plan you have selected, in addition to the price of the materials list. Please refer to the pricing schedule on our order form. **An Itemized Zip Quote is available for plans where you see this symbol.** ZIP

Bottom-Line Zip Quote

Option 2

The Bottom-Line Zip Quote is a one line summarized total cost for the home plan of your choice. This cost calculation is also based on the labor cost, material cost, and equipment cost (if applicable) within your zip code area. Bottom-Line Zip Quote is available for most plans. Please call for availability. The price of your initial Bottom-Line Zip Quote is $29.95. Each additional Bottom-Line Zip Quote ordered in conjunction with the initial order is only $14.95. A Bottom-Line Zip Quote may be purchased separately and does NOT have to be purchased in conjunction with a home plan order. **A Bottom-Line Zip Quote is available for all plans under 4,000 sq. ft. or where you see this symbol.** BL

*Please call for current availability.

The Itemized and Bottom-Line Zip Quotes give you approximated costs for constructing the particular house in your area. These costs are not exact and are only intended to be used as a preliminary estimate to help determine the affordability of a new home and/or as a guide to evaluate the general competitiveness of actual price quotes obtained through local suppliers and contractors. **Land, landscaping, sewer systems, site work, contractor overhead and profit, and other expenses are not included in our building cost figures. Excluding land and landscaping, you may incur an additional 20% to 40% in costs from the original estimate.** Garlinghouse and Marshall & Swift L.P. cannot guarantee any level of data accuracy or correctness in a Zip Quote and disclaim all liability for loss with respect to the same, in excess of the original purchase price of the Zip Quote product. All Zip Quote calculations are based upon the actual blueprints and do not reflect any differences or options that may be shown on the published house renderings, floor plans, or photographs.

CAD Files Now Available

A CAD file is available for plans where you see this symbol. CAD

Cad files are available in .dc5 or .dxf format or .dwg formats (R12, R13, R14, R2000). Please specify the file format at the time of your order. You will receive one bond set along with the CAD file when you place your order. **NOTE: CAD files are NOT returnable and can not be exchanged.**